Annual Report
Project and Readings
to accompany

Financial Accounting
Information for Decisions, 6e
Ingram • Albright

and

Financial Accounting
A Bridge to Decision Making, 6e
Ingram • Albright

Clayton A. Hock
Miami University

THOMSON
SOUTH-WESTERN

Australia · Brazil · Canada · Mexico · Singapore · Spain · United Kingdom · United States

THOMSON

SOUTH-WESTERN

Annual Report Project to accompany Financial Accounting: Information for Decisions, Sixth Edition
Robert W. Ingram and Thomas L. Albright

VP/Editorial Director:
Jack W. Calhoun

Publisher:
Rob Dewey

Executive Editor:
Sharon Oblinger

Developmental Editor:
Allison Rolfes

Marketing Manager:
Chris McNamee

Production Project Manager:
Tamborah Moore

Technology Project Editor:
Robin Browning

Web Coordinator:
Scott Cook

Manufacturing Coordinator:
Doug Wilke

Printer:
Globus
Minster, OH

Art Director:
Bethany Casey

Cover Designer:
Patti Hudepohl

Cover Image(s):
© Getty Images, Inc./The Image Bank
Collection/Photographer: Frank Pease

For permission to use material from this
text or product, submit a request online
at http://www.thomsonrights.com.

For more information about our
products, contact us at:

Thomson Learning Academic Resource
Center

1-800-423-0563

Thomson Higher Education
5191 Natorp Boulevard
Mason, OH 45040
USA

Table of Contents

Preface to the Student

The primary purpose of the **Annual Report Project** (**ARP**) is for you to gain experience with a company's financial statements, specifically the Annual Report to Stockholders and the Securities and Exchange Commission (SEC) Form 10-K Report. While portions of real financial statements are illustrated in the textbook, this project will put it all together. Your textbook and the **ARP** are integrated in their presentation and utilization of financial reports. The development and application of this approach to accounting should enhance your career.

Be aware that, occasionally, some of the ratio formulas you use in this project are slightly different from the basic ratio formulas used in the text. This is necessary because of the more complex data you will sometimes encounter in complete sets of a company's financial statements. When learning the basic formulas in a textbook setting, it is much easier for you to learn the underlying concepts if complicating factors are assumed away. When dealing with actual data, however, you must be able to incorporate the complexities or you risk arriving at an inappropriate conclusion. Part of the purpose of the **ARP** is to help you make that transition. When these slight modifications are introduced, the circumstances necessitating them are explained. The good news is that these modifications are usually very minor.

Another purpose of the **ARP** is to familiarize you with common sources of business and financial information. Employers will expect you to quickly and accurately obtain business and financial information about suppliers, customers, or competitors. Many of the assignments in this project will require you to use classic reference sources from the library or Internet that are used every day in the business world.

A third purpose of the **ARP** is to build teamwork skills. Many employers have made the remark, "Professors educate students one-at-a-time, but we employers work them in teams." Today, employers expect that you will have experience working closely on team-oriented projects. You may already know that teamwork skills take time and effort to develop. This is all part of your education, and failure to develop and extend your teamwork skills is just as dangerous to your career as failing to master personal computer and communication skills.

A fourth purpose of the **ARP** is to develop your writing skills, which is important for success in the business world. Depending on your professor's instructions, and based on your understanding and analysis of the material found in your annual report, you may prepare one of two written assignments:
1. write one shorter paper during the **ARP**—Assignment 7—and one longer paper at the end of the **ARP**—Assignment 15 entitled the Capstone Project; or
2. write a series of six short memos (one to three pages, or a length set by your professor) for Assignments 3, 6, 10, 12, 14 and 15—Optional Final Memo.

Introduction to Memos

Memos are a primary and effective means of communication within an organization. Generally, they are brief and to the point as busy executives do not have time to wade through long and rambling reports. Typically, memos have a beginning similar to the one illustrated below, which appears in the upper left-hand corner. Further, headings are often used to allow the reader to quickly determine the major points.

> Date memo is written.
>
> To: Person(s) to whom the memo is addressed.
> From: The person writing the memo.
> Subject: The purpose of the memo.
>
> ## Note
> Further discussion about writing memos can be found in Chapter 5 of *Essentials of Business Communications*, Seventh Edition, by Mary Ellen Guffey, ©2007, South-Western.

Based on different aspects of your **ARP** company, you will form opinions about the company which you may express in the form of a memo after Assignments 3, 6, 10, 12 and 14. Each memo is described in a double-lined box on the last page of these assignments and is another step in the development of your final memo for Assignment 15. To maintain a focus to your memos, the following scenario is provided.

> You are starting a firm to advise investors. A potential client has asked that you assist her in evaluating a company (your selected **ARP** company) which she might add to her investment portfolio. Also, based on the usefulness and quality of your memos and advice, she will determine whether or not to stay with your firm.

Your professor may prefer to develop another basis for writing the optional memos.

Preface to the Professor

The **ARP** has been used successfully in the sophomore-level introductory accounting course and in the MBA financial accounting course. It is the result of many years of experimentation with students—that they successfully make the transition from classroom topics and textbook examples to the use and understanding of *real* financial statements. The **ARP** (which includes analysis of the SEC 10-K and the proxy statement) is designed to achieve this. An unanticipated side benefit of this project has been that students enjoy dealing with *live* financial information.

It's often amazing how students will pore over the annual reports, proxy statements and SEC 10-Ks that they have received in the mail or downloaded from the Internet. When they run into complicated issues, their curiosity is piqued and they want to know more. Students are also intrigued by current readings. Each reading introduces an issue or issues related to the corresponding chapter of the text.

As in the Fifth Edition, Internet web sites have been integrated into the assignments where appropriate. All assignments, however, can still be completed using only traditional library resources.

Learning Groups. While this project is a valuable tool when completed by students working individually, its learning benefits are maximized when it is completed in groups. The strategy is to assign a different company to each group in the class. Each student obtains his/her own copies of the annual report, 10-K and proxy statement. The assigned company can then be used for a variety of in-class and out-of-class group-based assignments. Each group member is expected to become an expert regarding his/her company and then contribute that knowledge to a written report prepared by the group. Groups can also make end-of-semester class presentations based on their written report. All assignments can be used by either individuals or groups.

Assignment Options. Like the previous edition of the **ARP**, this one provides an alternative to the Capstone Project in Assignment 15—a series of six memos as part of Assignments 3, 6, 10, 12, 14 and 15—Optional Final Memo.

Some assignments ask the students to compare answers regarding their company with classmates. As an alternative, they may obtain the same information from other annual reports found on the Internet.

Both options are discussed in more detail in the *Instructor's Manual*.

The *Instructor's Manual* also provides a master list of the Dow 30 companies, the NYSE U.S. 100 Index, and the NASDAQ 100. Each company is identified by name and ticker symbol. The *Instructor's Manual* also includes a variety of hints and suggestions regarding use of the **ARP** (e.g., suggested guidelines about forming teams).

Thanks to many persons for their assistance in bringing this project to fruition. Students, for example, provided many helpful criticisms of early versions of many assignments. Faculty colleagues did the same. Special thanks to Allison Rolfes, Associate Developmental Editor of Thomson South-Western; Susan Hurst, Business Librarian at Miami University, who updated the library and Internet references; and Dr. Janel Bloch, who proofread portions of the accompanying *Instructor's Manual*. Special thanks also to Ethel Hock for formatting this Sixth Edition and preparing the camera-ready copy. All errors and omissions, however, are my personal responsibility.

I hope that you find this project helpful and useful. If you have suggestions for improvement, please call, write, or send e-mail. Your suggestions are welcome.

Clayton A. Hock
Department of Accountancy
Miami University
317-D Laws Hall
Oxford, OH 45056-1602

Phone: 513-529-6246
Fax: 513-529-4740
E-mail: hockca@muohio.edu

Summary of Ratio Formulas[*]

Ratio name	Formula	Measurement of
Accounts receivable turnover	$$\frac{\text{operating revenues (sales)}}{\text{accounts receivable}}$$	the ability to convert revenues to cash
Asset turnover	$$\frac{\text{sales}}{\text{total assets}}$$	the ability of assets to generate sales revenue
Current ratio	$$\frac{\text{total current assets}}{\text{total current liabilities}}$$	the ability to pay off current obligations as they come due
Debt to assets	$$\frac{\text{total debt}}{\text{total assets}}$$	the portion of assets that are provided by long-term creditors
Debt to equity	$$\frac{\text{total debt}}{\text{total stockholders' equity}}$$	the quantity of assets provided by long-term creditors compared to the quantity provided by owners
Dividend payout	$$\frac{\text{total cash dividends paid on common stock}}{\text{net income}}$$	the portion of net income distributed to stockholders in the form of dividends
Gross profit margin	$$\frac{\text{operating revenues (sales) - cost of goods sold}}{\text{operating revenues}}$$	efficiency in production or purchase of goods for sale
Inventory turnover	$$\frac{\text{cost of goods sold}}{\text{inventory}}$$	success in selling inventory
Market value to book value	$$\frac{\text{market value per (common) share}}{\text{book value per (common) share}}$$	investors' confidence in ability of management to deploy the company's resources profitably
Operating cash flow to total assets	$$\frac{\text{cash from operations}}{\text{total assets}}$$	effectiveness in using the company's assets to generate cash flow from operating activities
Operating profit margin	$$\frac{\text{operating revenues - all operating expenses}}{\text{operating revenues}}$$	efficiency of the company's primary, or central, activities
Profit margin	$$\frac{\text{net income}}{\text{operating revenues (sales)}}$$	ability to produce profits from sales
Return on assets	$$\frac{\text{net income}}{\text{total assets}}$$	the ability to generate profit from the investment in assets
Return on common equity	$$\frac{\text{net income (- preferred dividends, if any)}}{\text{common stockholders' equity}}$$	return earned on capital invested by the firm's common stockholders

[*]Ratio formulas vary from analyst to analyst. These commonly used versions are used in the *Annual Report Project*.

Assignment 1
Choosing a Company and
Securing Its Annual Report

The purpose of the **Annual Report Project** (**ARP**) is to apply the lessons of your accounting course to a real company. You will discover how the issues, topics, practices and procedures described in your textbook actually affect a company's financial statements. You will conduct library and/or Internet research to familiarize yourself with your company and the industry in which your firm competes. Later in the course you will begin to analyze and evaluate your individual firm's financial stability and trends.

Your company may be assigned to you by your professor or your professor may allow you to choose your own company. However your company is chosen, it will be the basis for this **ARP**.

The company should be publically traded, i.e., its stock is traded on a stock exchange such as the New York Stock Exchange (NYSE). It is usually best to avoid financial institutions, e.g., banks or insurance companies, as well as public utilities, because these companies normally have specialized accounting practices. Your professor may give you additional guidelines on choosing a company.

Identifying Companies from Which to Choose

Recognizing that your professor may have placed some limitations on your choice, you may want to narrow your choice further by selecting an industry that interests you for one or more reasons, such as:

1. You, or someone you know, has worked in a particular industry about which you would like to learn more.

2. A company in that industry is located in your hometown or in a nearby location.

3. You regularly purchase products from that industry (e.g., textbooks, clothing, or beverages).

4. The industry might provide employment opportunities after graduation.

5. The industry has been in the news lately, and you are interested in being better informed about the issues that were raised.

Library Resources

A good place to start is in your school's library. Following are five sources that provide information about many industries and specific information about individual firms in those industries.

1. *Standard & Poor's Industry Surveys*, published by Standard & Poor's, Inc. This three-volume document is published every quarter and updated twice a year. It covers approximately 52 industries and more than 1,200 companies. In the front of each volume you will find a section entitled the "Index to Companies." This section lists all of the industry categories and each of the companies within each industry.

2. *Value Line Investment Survey*, published by Value Line, Inc. This service is updated weekly and comes in three parts. The front page of Part 1, "Summary & Index," lists more than 90 industry categories along with the page number where information on each industry can be found. In Part 3 you will find the industry information as well as specific information about each company in each industry.

3. *Fortune* is a bi-weekly business magazine published by AOL Time Warner. Its annual mid-April listing of the 500 largest firms in the United States is referred to as the Fortune 500 and is probably the most widely cited listing of this type.

4. *Hoover's Handbook of American Business,* published by Hoover's, Inc., profiles 750 major U.S. companies, including overview, history, officers, location, products, and competitors.

5. *North American Industry Classification System: United States*, published by the U.S. Government Office of Management & Budget, organizes all businesses and industries in the United States into six-digit NAICS codes. In the back of the volume is an alphabetical index of industry categories with the NAICS code for each category. The front of the manual has a detailed description of each industry category. Use this manual to select an industry and its six-digit NAICS code. After selecting an industry, go to the *Million Dollar Directory*, published by Dun & Bradstreet, Inc. The directory is a series of five volumes; look for the one labeled "Series Cross-Reference Industrial Classification." This volume is organized by NAICS code numbers. You will find many companies for whatever NAICS code you have chosen along with each firm's mailing address and telephone number.

For a detailed explanation of NAICS codes, see page 15.

Internet Resources

The following sites on the Internet are a rich source of financial information.

1. www.nyse.com (New York Stock Exchange) – Click on "Listed Company Directory."

2. www.nasdaq.com (National Association of Securities Dealers Automated Quotation)

3. www.amex.com (American Stock Exchange) – Lists over 800 companies. Click on "Equities" and then "Listed Company Directory."

4. www.forbes.com – Click on "lists" and use "400 Best Big Companies"

Group Project
(If you are not part of a group, skip to Obtaining Financial Statements.)

If your group is to evaluate several firms in the same industry, your first task will be to assign a specific company to each member of your group. This will be your first exercise in group decision making.

Each group member is expected to become very knowledgeable regarding one or all of your team's assigned companies. You will obtain the company's financial statements and observe how your firm implements the principles and practices that you will learn in this course. If team members have been assigned a different firm, the other members of your group will be doing the same thing for their firms (which compete with yours).

Each member will contribute his/her expertise regarding the assigned firm(s) to the group's report, which will be due on a date set by your professor. If your professor requires you to complete Assignment 15, there are more instructions on the group report and analysis in the Assignment. You should review those instructions *very soon* and begin to develop strategies for completion of the project.

First, however, complete the following steps.

1. Choose a name for your group and write it in the space below. Feel free to be creative. For example, you might want to select a name that is a clever play-on-words regarding the name of your company or industry. Your professor will probably appreciate the humor.

   Group name _____

2. List each person in your group with telephone number and e-mail address.

Group Member Names	Phone Numbers	E-mail Addresses
a. _____	_____	_____
b. _____	_____	_____
c. _____	_____	_____
d. _____	_____	_____
e. _____	_____	_____
f. _____	_____	_____

3. Turn in one copy of the group information to your professor.

Obtaining Financial Statements

Most future assignments will be based on information contained in your company's Annual Report, its SEC Form 10-K, and its proxy statement. You will need to secure the most recent copy of the these items.

The Annual Report is a document that must be distributed to all shareholders every year. It contains the firm's financial statements as well as a variety of other required and optional information. Often it is a slick and glossy publication with color pictures of the executives, company facilities, and products. The SEC Form 10-K is the version of the annual report that must be filed annually with the Securities and Exchange Commission (SEC), an agency of the federal government in Washington, D.C. When you secure your firm's Annual Report and SEC 10-K you will notice that the two documents have many similarities but that they also have some striking differences.

The proxy statement is a document describing matters that will be discussed or voted on at the annual stockholders' meeting. It is also the device by which management of the corporation solicits your authorization (proxy) to vote your shares on its behalf. Of greatest interest, perhaps, is that proxy statements must provide detailed information about compensation of key executive personnel. (Ever wonder how much money the president of a large corporation is paid?)

Obtaining the Required Materials from the Company

1. Contact your company directly by telephone, letter, or e-mail. You will need to go to your university library, community public library, or the Internet to obtain this information. The address, and usually the phone number, can be obtained from the following sources:

    a. *LexisNexis Corporate Affiliations*, LexisNexis.

    b. *Million Dollar Directory*, Dun & Bradstreet.

    c. *Mergent Online*, Mergent.

    d. *Hoover's MasterList of U.S. Companies*, Hoover's, Inc.

    e. The company's web site, usually the company's name followed by ".com." Once at the company's homepage, click under a heading such as *Investor Services* or *Investor Relations* for details on ordering annual reports.

2. The following hints will help you secure the necessary materials.

    a. Companies usually have an Office of Investor Relations or Shareholder Relations. Write to, or telephone, that office. If your company has an Internet homepage, you may be able to send an e-mail request directly.

    b. Explain that you are a student at (identify your school) and that as part of an accounting class assignment this term you will be studying the firm and its financial information.

c. Request a copy of the firm's most recent Annual Report, most recent SEC Form 10-K, and its most recent proxy statement. Most firms are happy to provide these documents. They tend to think of you either as a potential investor, potential customer, or both.

d. Provide an *exact* mailing address.

3. Note the following information regarding your request.

a. Method of making the request (e.g., telephone, fax, letter, e-mail)

_____

b. Post office address or e-mail address of firm (if you sent a letter or e-mail)

_____

_____

_____

c. Phone number of firm (if you telephoned or faxed) _____

d. Date of request for documents _____

Obtaining the Required Materials from the Company's Web site

Though having a real "glossy" annual report and proxy statement would be preferable, it is not always possible to get one in a timely manner. Therefore, you may want to consider securing your company's annual report and proxy from the Internet.

When obtaining your annual report from your company's web site, it is not necessary to download and print the entire report, which can reach nearly 100 pages in length. Since only a portion of the annual report will be used consistently, it is suggested that you print only the following: (a) Management Discussion and Analysis (MD&A), (b) financial statements, and (3) notes to financial statements. During the **ARP** the other sections of the annual report will be referred to only once or twice or not at all. Any information needed from these sections can be secured by scrolling through the annual report.

Sample Letter

If you prefer to write a letter it could be similar to the one on the following page.

Later Assignments

In later assignments you will compare information about your company with information from the annual reports of your classmates or from annual reports found on the Internet.

Sample Letter

(Your Name and Address)

(Today's Date)

Investor Relations Department
Humble Pie Bakery Corporation
3652 Modesty Boulevard
Ovenhot, Arizona 00000

Director of Investor Relations:

I am a student at (name your school). As part of an accounting class assignment this term I will be examining and analyzing the financial reports of a major corporation.

I have chosen your firm and would like to study the financial reports of your corporation as part of my class assignment. Would you please assist me by sending me a copy of your most recent Annual Report, most recent SEC 10-K, and most recent Proxy Statement? Thank you very much for your help!

Sincerely,

(Signature)

(Your Name, typed)

Name _____   Professor _____

Course _____   Section _____

Completing Assignment 1 – Choosing a Company

1. What is the name of the company you have chosen?

   _____

2. Which industry category does your firm represent?

   _____

3. Write several paragraphs describing how (and why) you chose the firm you did. Did you use any of the resources listed earlier in this assignment, or the Internet? Were they easy to use? Hard to use? Which one(s) would you recommend to friends if they had to complete this assignment? Discuss.

   Note: *Please think and plan carefully before writing. Readability, spelling, organization, grammar, and sentence structure will all be considered in grading your response.*

   _____

   _____

   _____

   _____

   _____

   _____

   _____

   _____

   _____

   _____

   _____

   _____

   _____

   _____

   _____

Assignment 2
Understanding Your Company
and Its Environment

A company's financial statements are best understood when the reader understands the company and comprehends fully the environment in which the firm operates: economic, social, legal and political. The purpose of this assignment is to gain an understanding of selected factual aspects of your company. You will read an article about your company, which may reveal a shakeup of key management personnel or new product development, and read an article about your company's current environment. There may be important new legislation that has affected your firm. Additionally, new technology, new competitors, new social trends, or legal battles could all affect the general health of your firm.

Key References for this Assignment

The following are excellent sources of background information on companies and/or industries. If some of the suggested references are not available in your library, your reference librarian may be able to suggest other sources that you could use instead. In addition, almost every industry has a periodical, such as *Progressive Grocer* or *Advertising Age*, which would be a good source of information about issues facing the industry.

1. *Standard & Poor's Industry Surveys*, published by Standard & Poor's, Inc. This three-volume document is published every quarter and updated twice a year. It covers approximately 52 industries and more than 1,200 companies.

2. *Value Line Investment Survey*, published by Value Line, Inc. This weekly service is comprised of three sections. The "Summary and Index" (Part 1) lists the page numbers in Part 3 where information regarding your industry category can be found. The *Value Line Investment Survey* provides detailed reports on approximately 1,700 companies across more than 90 industry groups.

3. *Encyclopedia of American Industries*, published by Gale Research. Provides detailed, comprehensive information on a wide range of industries in every realm of American business.

4. *The Corporate Directory of U.S. Public Companies*, Walker's Western Research, provides brief company descriptions and financial data, along with contact information, NAICS codes, names of key officers, etc.

5. *Mergent Industrial Manual* (or Transportation, Public Utilities, or Bank & Finance manuals), Mergent Inc. Print materials include financial data, corporate overviews, and contact data. The online version (available at your library) is excellent for detailed financial data, annual reports, and links to SEC filings.

6. *Standard & Poor's Register of Corporations, Directors and Executives*, published by Standard & Poor's (S&P). This three volume set covers over 75,000 corporations and profiles 350,000 executives.

7. *Standard & Poor's Corporation Records*, published by Standard & Poor's. Information on U.S. and international companies includes full income statements and balance sheets, extensive corporate profiles, and recent news.

8. *Standard & Poor's 500 Guide*, published by Standard & Poor's. Corporate information and financial statement statistics are provided by the components of the S&P 500 Index.

9. *LexisNexis Corporate Affiliations*, published by the LexisNexis Group. This is a good source to determine if your company is publicly or privately owned, or a subsidiary of a larger parent company. This eight volume set also includes information on international corporations.

10. *America's Corporate Families*, published by Dun & Bradstreet, Inc. Volume I provides detailed information on all "ultimate" parent companies. Volume II cross-references the "ultimate" parent company and its subsidiaries.

11. *Hoover's*, published by Hoover's, Inc., has both print and online materials that include histories, financial data, and lists of competitors. *Hoover's Online* (www.hoovers.com) has some free information, and if your library subscribes, you can access more data, including industry comparisons of financial ratios.

12. *Marketline Business Information Centre* is an online database that includes 10,000 U.S. and international company profiles providing company overviews, history, key executives, competitors, and SWOT analyses. Industry and country reports are also available, giving you more information about the operating environment as well.

13. *Business Source Premier* by Ebsco and *ABI Inform* by Proquest are also online databases. They include citations and many full-text articles in both popular and scholarly business journals.

14. *Business Periodicals Index*, published by H.W. Wilson Company, is a print index that will lead you to articles published in business journals about your company or industry.

15. *The New York Times Index*, New York Times Company, will let you find specific articles in *The New York Times* about your company or industry. You can then ask your librarian about the best way to locate the full-text articles.

16. *The Wall Street Journal Index*, Dow Jones & Company, will let you find specific articles in *The Wall Street Journal* about your company or industry. You can then ask your librarian about the best way to locate the full-text articles.

On the Internet

If you don't already know your company's stock ticker symbol, a one-to-five letter code under which the company's stock trades on the stock exchange, go to:
www2.barchart.com/lookup.asp or **finance.yahoo.com**

Name _____   Professor _____

Course _____   Section _____

Completing Assignment 2 – Understanding Your Company

1. Use the Key References listed on pages 9 and 10 or the Internet to obtain the information requested below and to answer the questions that follow. Most companies' web sites are the "company name.com," e.g., Staples is Staples.com and Coca-cola is Coca-cola.com. The Web site can also be found through a search engine such as Google.

    Note: *Please think and plan carefully before answering the questions. Readability, organization, spelling, grammar, and sentence structure will all be considered in grading your responses.*

    a. Basic company facts:

    Complete name of firm _____

    Stock ticker symbol _____

    Stock exchange where traded _____

    Primary and secondary NAICS (or SIC) codes _____

    State of incorporation _____

    Year of incorporation _____

    Independent auditor _____

    Company's fiscal year-end (month and day) _____

    Web site _____

    b. List up to five products your company produces (manufacturing company) or sells (retailing company) and customers to whom those products are probably sold.

Product	Customer
_____	_____
_____	_____
_____	_____
_____	_____
_____	_____

    c. The size of a company is determined by more than one factor. For those factors listed, enter the amount or number for your company.

    Note: *For a better analysis of your company's size, it would be best to compare your company's numbers with the industry average, if available.*

11

Dollar amount of assets $ _____

Dollar amount of sales/revenues $ _____

Net income $ _____

Number of products/services   _____

Earnings per share (diluted) $ _____

Number of common shares outstanding   _____

Other measures:

_____   _____

_____   _____

Based on the numbers listed above, would your company be classified as large? Briefly discuss.

_____

_____

_____

_____

_____

_____

_____

_____

d. Each public company is required to have a Board of Directors (BD) and often there is a picture of the BD near the end of the annual report. Relative to your company's BD, complete the following:

Total number of individuals serving on the BD: _____

Composition of BD by gender: male _____   female _____

Composition of BD by ethnic group: African American _____

    Asian _____   Caucasian _____   Other _____

How many members are "independent," i.e., have no official relationship/ position with the company? _____

How many members are "insiders," i.e., hold a position within the company, e.g., treasurer? _____

Would you say that your company's BD is diversified? Why?

_____

_____

_____

How would describe the average age of the BD? _____

_____

_____

2. Use the Key References listed on pages 9 and 10 to identify two recent articles (no more than two years old), one about your firm and another about its industry. Photocopy (or download and print) them to turn in with this assignment. Only one article may be from the Internet.

    Note: *It is a serious breach of academic integrity to tear articles out of magazines that do not belong to you, e.g., those in the library. Please don't do it!*

    a. The first article looks at your company. Various facts, allegations, successes and failures about a company are often the focus of articles in the business and popular press. These articles should be more objective and provide a perspective other than management's point of view.

    Search method

        Key Reference _____ Edition _____

        Web site _____

    Author _____

    Title _____

    Name of periodical or Web site _____

    Date of periodical _____

    Page numbers (normally not available on an Internet source) _____

    Describe why this article is significant and interesting. Limit your response to no more than 100 words and use complete sentences.

_____

_____

_____

_____

_____

_____

_____

_____

_____

_____

b. To further your understanding of your company, the second article focuses on the industry of which your firm is a part. Overall trends within an industry generally have a large impact on the success of specific firms within the industry. Through your search process, you will gain some insight into the nature of the industry in which your firm competes.

Search method

  Key Reference _____ Edition _____

  Web site _____

Author _____

Title _____

Name of periodical or Web site _____

Date of periodical _____

Page numbers (Normally not available on an Internet source) _____

Describe why this article is significant and interesting. Limit your response to no more than 100 words and use complete sentences.

_____

_____

_____

_____

_____

_____

_____

_____

_____

_____

3. What are the two most interesting aspects of your company (or its industry) that you have discovered so far? Briefly comment on them.

  a. _____

  _____

  b. _____

  _____

The North American Industry Classification System (NAICS)

The North American Industry Classification System (NAICS, pronounced "nakes") has replaced the U.S. Standard Industrial Classification Code (SIC Code). NAICS was developed by the U.S., Canada and Mexico after the North American Free Trade Agreement (NAFTA). The NAICS reclassifies and regroups industries to better reflect the North American economy, now more service oriented and technological than manufacturing based, i.e., process rather than product.

The NAICS codes contain six digits rather than the SIC Codes four. The first two, like the SIC Codes, represent the general economic sector in which the industry is classified. The third designates the subsector; the fourth the industry group; and the fifth the NAICS industry. The sixth digit is unique in that it refers to the specific country's industry.

Though NAICS is said to be a better classification system, conversion to its use has been slow. A major problem is that approximately half of the industries in the manufacturing sector of NAICS do not have comparable industries in the SIC system, impacting comparability of current and historic data. While the Annual Census of Manufactures has used only the NAICS Codes since 1998, the SEC's EDGAR database continued to use SIC Codes.

On the Internet

More information about the NAICS can be found on the Internet at:

www.naics.com (NAICS Association web site)

or

www.census.gov/epcd/www/naics.html

Reading 2
Revenge of the Bean Counters

By Daren Fonda
With reporting by Dody Tsiantar and
Adam Zagorin

No longer frail in the face of fraud, accounting firms are thriving on new laws that give them real clout

There's a joke in the accounting trade that the difference between a wobbly grocery cart and a corporate auditor is that the cart has a mind of its own. Very funny, unless you had invested in MCI (formerly WorldCom), which recently announced that the pre-tax income it reported for 2000 and 2001 was just a tad off— $74.4 billion less than it had said, after write-downs and adjustments. Outside auditors have signed off on bogus earnings reports and balance sheets at companies from Rite Aid to Xerox. In some cases, auditors dealt with corporate brass intent on concealing thievery; World-Com's ex-CFO, Scott Sullivan, recently pleaded guilty to fraud and conspiracy charges, for instance. In other cases, auditors simply lacked spine: again and again, they failed to police the books aggressively for fear of losing the client, along with consulting gigs that brought in higher profits than standard audit work.

The tables have turned. Strengthened and emboldened by the Sarbanes-Oxley Act, which overhauled accounting responsibilities, the bean counters have taken off their kid gloves and snapped on rubber ones. With their federally issued mandate to look for trouble, accountants no longer have to take a company's word that its audit policies are legit. The accountants have the power to challenge corporate ledgers with impunity—and they're raking in money doing so. "Auditors and audit committees are now in the catbird seat," says Harvard Business School professor Jay Lorsch. Companies no longer feel free to dump their auditors, for fear of sparking a public spat; no one wants to spook jittery investors, provoke shareholder lawsuits or another regulatory crackdown.

Accountants are challenging corporate ledgers with impunity—and they're raking in money doing so

"There's more respect for the auditor," says Julie Lindy, editor of Bowman's Accounting Report. "Companies no longer think the audit process is about creating the illusion that they're jumping through hoops."

The change in the relationship is largely because of Sarbanes-Oxley, known in the trade as Sox or Sarbox. The 2002 law stiffens accountants' spines in part because it places them under a new federal watchdog agency that will soon start spot-checking their work. That agency, the Public Company Accounting Oversight Board, also has an industry moniker— Peek-a-Boo—and recently issued a stricter set of rules detailing how auditors should evaluate internal controls. Companies must test these controls regularly, and such tests must be conducted by a firm different from the company's outside auditor, to avoid conflicts of interest. The agency's chairman, former New York Federal Reserve Bank chief William McDonough, is close to finalizing joint supervision rules with the European Union— welcome news to U.S. investors after the collapse of Parmalat, the Italian firm that had concealed $18 billion in debt.

Bottom line: Be nice to your accountants—or else. Outside auditors answer to an audit committee made up of at least two independent board members; previously they might have dealt only with a chief financial officer, and "it would not have been unusual for CFOs ... to try to limit the scope of an audit," says Scott Green, head of compliance for the law firm Weil, Gotshal & Manges. Since the law bars accounting firms from selling certain consulting services to audit clients, including such lucrative ones as information-systems design, auditors face less pressure from their partners to pass cooked books.

The new measures have "put the fear of God" in corporate bosses and their employees "to make sure that auditors get accurate information," says Edward Nusbaum, CEO of Grant Thornton, the nation's sixth largest accounting firm. Gary Shamis, a managing partner at SS&G Financial Services in Cleveland, Ohio, says he recently met with the audit committee of a client "for the first time in 20 years." Because auditors are under greater scrutiny and because the law demands it, they must also document the process more meticulously.

And so the fee meter is running. The death of the Arthur Andersen firm, which dissolved after being found guilty of obstructing justice in the Enron case, reduced the Big Five accounting firms to the Final Four. That in part is why audit fees for FORTUNE 500 companies are expected to climb 38% this year, according to a survey by the Public Accounting Report. Top lines for accounting firms already look healthier. Ernst & Young booked a 17.4% revenue increase in its 2003 fiscal year, to $5.3 billion. Grant Thornton booked a 21% increase, to $485 million. The other winners? Smaller shops, which are absorbing business that the big audit firms are barred from providing, such as running tests of

internal controls for clients. "The environment for these services is phenomenally good," says Stephen Giusto, CFO of Resources Connection, an accountancy and consulting company based in Costa Mesa, Calif., whose fiscal 2003 revenues rose 11%, to $202 million.

38%
The increase in audit fees paid by the largest companies

9.1 %
Net revenue increase of the top seven accounting firms

35,000
Number of hours big companies expect it will take to comply with just one part of Sarbanes-Oxley

Sources: *Public Accounting Report*, Financial Executives International

---

Of course, with the bean counters cashing in, the expense side of the ledger is going up for clients. The largest U.S. companies will typically spend more than $4.6 million each to comply with just one section of the law, according to Financial Executives International. And large companies complain that the get-tough accounting regimen is draining resources. Paul Schmidt,

controller for General Motors, says GM's audit committee meets "six to seven times face to face and four to five times by teleconference" annually. The "bigger drain," says Schmidt, is that GM's chairman and CFO are spending more time on accounting and certification issues, "instead of on strategy."

Watchdog groups, on the other hand, say some of the changes imposed by Sox are toothless. When Congress was drafting the law, "the accounting firms worked hard to minimize its scope," says Barbara Roper of the Consumer Federation of America. Unlike the mutual-fund and securities industries, she says, "the accounting profession never really acknowledged that there was a serious problem with the way it did business."

But having paid out huge settlements to the angry shareholders of their crooked clients, the accountants know whom they really work for. And now they really do have something in common with wobbly shopping carts: they're both hard to push around.

Time
March 29, 2004
pp. 38 - 39

Questions for Consideration

1. What were some of the events that triggered the Sarbanes-Oxley Act of 2002? Explain.

2. Sarbanes-Oxley, in part, reduced the responsibilities of the accounting profession and changed its relationship with the company's audit committee. What responsibilities were affected and how has the relationship with the audit committee changed? How has the profession benefitted? Discuss.

Name _____   Professor _____

Course _____   Section _____

Assignment 3
Initial Review of the Annual Report

By now you should have the annual report, SEC 10-K and proxy statement of your company, whether you requested them from the company or obtained them on the Internet. The purpose of this assignment is to review and understand the basic information that is reported in your company's annual report, except the financial statements and the footnotes to the financial statements.

Organization of the Annual Report

In general, you will find annual reports organized into the six different sections discussed below in their typical order.

1. **Financial Highlights** – A summary covering as many as 10 or 20 years. Often this section contains a variety of charts and graphs which provide a shorthand summary of the firm over a number of years.

2. **The Company and Its Products** – A fairly lengthy section, mostly public relations-type information. It's where the company brags about its products, people, and activities. There may be lots of color pictures of the executives if the company had a good year. However, if the company had a bad year, there may be no pictures of the executives at all.

3. **Management's Discussion and Analysis** – often referred to in the business press by its initials, the MD&A. Here management is required to identify significant events, trends and developments affecting the firm and to discuss management's thinking on these matters.

4. **Financial Statements** and the **Notes to the Financial Statements** – Following the MD&A, you should find the financial statements and the accompanying notes. Financial statements will be analyzed more throughly in Assignments 4 and 5; footnotes will be studied in Assignment 8.

5. **Statement of Management Responsibility** and the **Report of the Independent Accountants (or Auditor's Report)** – Read these carefully as they reveal (1) who is responsible for the content of the financial statements and (2) whether the financial statements present fairly the financial situation of the firm.

6. **Basic Company Facts** – Usually two or three pages listing, for example, the officers and directors, stock exchange listing, and state of incorporation.

Completing the Assignment

Name of your company _____

1. Use the Financial Highlights section of your company's annual report to note the following information.

Item	most recent year	next most recent year	next most recent year	next most recent year
Net income	$ _____	$ _____	$ _____	$ _____
Total assets	$ _____	$ _____	$ _____	$ _____
Total liabilities	$ _____	$ _____	$ _____	$ _____
Long-term debt	$ _____	$ _____	$ _____	$ _____
Dividend per share	$ _____	$ _____	$ _____	$ _____
Earnings/share (basic EPS)	$ _____	$ _____	$ _____	$ _____

2. From Management's Discussion and Analysis (MD&A), answer the following.

   a. Does your company's MD&A have the following major sections?

   Note: *All companies may not have these sections or use this exact terminology.*

	Yes	No
Overview	_____	_____
Results of operations	_____	_____
Financial condition and liquidity	_____	_____
Market risk management	_____	_____
Critical accounting policies	_____	_____
Caution concerning forward-looking information	_____	_____
Other _____	_____	_____

   b. What is the general tone of management's comments in this section? Was the most recent year a positive or negative experience for the company? Is management optimistic or pessimistic about the future. Discuss.

   _____

   _____

   _____

   _____

_____

_____

_____

_____

3. Locate the Statement of Management Responsibility and the Report of the Independent Accountants (or Auditor's Report) and read them carefully to answer the following questions.

   a. Who is responsible for the preparation and content of the financial statements?

   _____

   b. Does the company have an audit committee? _____ Yes _____ No
   If your company does not have an audit committee go to question d.

   c. What is (are) the responsibility(s) of the audit committee?

   _____

   _____

   _____

   d. What type of system has management established to produce reliable financial statements?

   _____

   e. Which financial statements are covered by the audit report?

   _____

   _____

   _____

   _____

   f. Who is responsible for assessing that the financial statements are fairly presented?

   _____

   g. To whom is the audit report addressed?

   _____

   h. Did your firm receive an unqualified opinion? _____ Yes _____ No
   (See note on page 22.)

> **Note**
> The most common opinions expressed by auditors about the
> financial statements are:
> ▸ **unqualified**, which means that the financial statements con-
>   form to GAAP and are fairly presented;
> ▸ **qualified**, which means that except for the qualified item the
>   financial statements conform to GAAP and are fairly presented;
> ▸ **disclaimer**, which means that the auditor does not express an
>   opinion.

    i. If your firm did **not** receive an unqualified opinion, what reason(s) was
        (were) given?

_____

_____

_____

_____

_____

4. Review the Basic Company Facts to find the following information. Note,
    however, that some companies may disclose some of this information in
    another part of the annual report.

    a. Name of CEO _____

    b. Name of Chairman of the Board _____

    c. When will the annual stockholders' meeting be held? _____

    d. Where will the annual stockholders' meeting be held? _____

    e. Does your company have a:

        direct stock purchase plan? _____ Yes _____ No

        dividend reinvestment plan? _____ Yes _____ No

    f. What company serves as the Transfer Agent? _____

    g. List other interesting information/facts, if any, disclosed in this section?

_____

_____

_____

_____

_____

_____

5. Optional Memo No. 1 – Company Background

Having completed the first three assignments of **The Annual Report Project**, you have acquired sufficient information about your company and its industry to prepare the first memo to your client.

For format see page -vi- in the Preface or follow your professor's instructions.

Guide for Memo No. 1

State your *initial reaction*, i.e., favorable or unfavorable. In your analysis you may want to consider the following:

    a. your company's industry;

    b. its major products or services;

    c. general economic and political environment;

    d. your company's position in the industry, i.e., does it appear to be a leader (pro-active) or follower (reactionary); and

    e. assessment of the non-financial information contained in your company's annual report.

Reading 3
Not Just Comment Letters:
How the FASB's Constituents Can Participate in Its Processes

The FASB's role in the capital markets can be simply stated: To serve the investing public by developing high quality financial reporting standards that result in credible, transparent financial information. But the Board's goal of providing high quality financial reporting standards would be out of reach without the active participation of the FASB's constituents—companies, auditors and users of financial information—in the standard-setting process. As we discuss in this article, constituent participation is woven into the very fabric of the FASB's processes, but the opportunities for all constituents to take part may not be fully appreciated by all.

The Importance of Due Process

The process of developing financial reporting standards involves many steps. It starts with gaining an understanding of the economic substance of the transactions to which a proposed standard will apply and ends with the issuance of an accounting standard. Along the way, the Board continuously assesses how its proposals would change current practice—in particular, whether the benefits of the proposed accounting will exceed the costs of implementing it. The many steps involved in developing accounting standards and assessing their effectiveness is called "due process."

And such due process is no empty formula: it is essential if the FASB is to successfully carry out its mission. As Mitchell Danaher, Assistant Comptroller at General Electric Company and a frequent participant in FASB activities, comments, "A standard is only as good as the information upon which its development is based." Since the only way to get the best information is to collect it "on the ground," from the constituents who have it and who have to use the standard, their participation is indispensable. As Danaher aptly says, "Good standard setting is all about communication."

Advisory Councils and Project Resource Groups

The Board has several different formal channels for gathering input, including its Financial Accounting Standards Advisory Council (FASAC), User Advisory Council (UAC) and newly formed Small Business Advisory Committee. Moreover, an important first step for any major Board project is the formation of an advisory group, called a Project Resource Group, that includes representatives from each of the Board's major constituencies—users of financial statements, preparers and auditors.

Janet Pegg, a Senior Managing Director at Bear Stearns and a member of four FASB Project Resource Groups (Business Combinations, Performance Reporting, Revenue Recognition and Share-Based Compensation) as well as the FASAC and the UAC, puts it this way: "The Board is continuing to reach out to the user community, and the Advisory Councils are a key component."

Project Resource Group members are selected based on their expertise with the transactions under study. Their role is to provide information and practical insights from a constituents' perspective. For example, in the early stages of the business combinations project, the Board solicited feedback from constituents about the difficulties they were having in understanding and applying the purchase method of accounting. That feedback helped the Board identify the particular aspects of the accounting for business combinations that needed improvement or clarification, guiding its decisions about the scope and direction that project should take.

Jan Hauser, a PricewaterhouseCoopers partner and Business Combinations Project Resource Group member, notes the diversity of participants and the free exchange of ideas that occur in meetings with the Board and staff: "Board members, other Project Resource Group members, preparers, users, analysts, accounting firms and the SEC were all involved. We met to explore ideas and comment on the direction the Board was taking, not to give an official response. I feel it's really critical that this kind of interaction happens before the exposure draft stage."

In addition to participating in formal meetings, Project Resource Group members serve as a source of information and a sounding board for the FASB staff when conducting basic accounting research. It is not uncommon for FASB staff members to approach Project Resource Group members individually on particular questions. For example, members of the Business Combination Project Resource Group were asked by telephone or e-mail to comment on issues related to accounting for in-process research and development and on proposed changes to the definition of a business. As Ms. Pegg explains, "We're expected to be available to the staff to pick our brains and to give our reaction to in-process decisions." Her conclusion? "The Project Resource Groups are helping forge a stronger relationship between the FASB and the analyst community, resulting in much higher quality accounting standards from an analyst's point of view."

Conversely, Project Resource Group members are strongly committed to reaching out to practitioners so that they can present the FASB with informed opinion. As Ms. Pegg notes, "In my work at Bear Stearns, I'm constantly encouraging my colleagues to offer their input themselves because the FASB wants it."

At PricewaterhouseCoopers,

Ms. Hauser explains, "If a client has an issue and asks how they can comment, we will make an introductory call to FASB, which the client can then follow up. I encourage clients to do this in writing, then offer to follow through with a conversation. Over and above that, we have an outreach program to various industry groups. Designated partners in such sectors as insurance, technology and utilities liaise with clients and other engagement teams to get their feedback when they see an EITF or FASB issue that might have an impact on a particular group."

Other Means of Input

Project Resource Groups are critical, but they're far from the only means at the FASB's disposal to learn the views of its constituents. Some of the most important are the following:

• *Liaison Groups.* The FASB maintains relations with more than two dozen industry groups, from the American Bankers Association to the National Association of College and University Business Officers, meeting with them regularly throughout the year to gain insight into particular sectors' reactions to Board decisions. When even more direct input is needed, the Board will conduct field visits with preparers and users, providing the Board with the benefit of their expertise in assessing feasibility of proposed rules.

• *Public Access to Meetings and Information.* Meetings of the FASB, and other FASB groups and committees, including Project Resource Groups, normally are open to public observation, under the Board's Rules of Pro-

cedure. FASAC and UAC meetings are also open to the public. Additionally, the FASB website, www.fasb.org, is a rich source of information about tentative decisions on all the Board's projects.

• *Roundtables on Exposure Drafts.* After an exposure draft is issued, the Board often holds public roundtable meetings to bring together the best thinking on the exposure draft topic across the entire constituent community. To take one recent example, last August a Roundtable on the exposure draft of an amendment to FASB Statement 140, *Qualifying Special-Purpose Entities and Isolation of Transferred Assets*, drew 26 experts from private industry, major law firms, investment banking firms, the major auditing firms, industry liaison groups and the SEC for a full-day discussion of issues of constituent concern. Some participants agreed to assist the FASB in gathering further information.

• *Letters.* You don't have to belong to the FASAC or the UAC or even visit the FASB in Norwalk to make a contribution. Board meetings are now available by audio webcast and, as in the past, telephone. The Board welcomes communication from any interested member of the public about its deliberations at any stage. Constituents should not think that they can only express their views to the FASB in comment letters on exposure drafts. As Mitch Danaher puts it, "Any company can participate directly in the development of new standards. If you have some insight to offer on the standard or there is a provision that is unclear to you, send a letter or e-mail to the FASB. Board members read all the comment letters they receive. Be specific, be clear and be timely." Jan Hauser agrees: "Articulate your concerns, suggest how the proposed standard can be better crafted, explain any problems you see, offer a better solution if you have one, and the Board and staff will be receptive to your input."

Conclusion: Just Do It
According to Janet Pegg, "It's our duty as analysts to let the Board know what we think." To Mitch Danaher, it's also a matter of self-interest. "Companies that leave it to others to review and comment on proposed standards are taking a leap of faith that others will communicate to the Board on their issues. It is in everyone's best interest that all issues are identified and addressed before a standard is finalized. You can't assume that someone else will do it on your behalf." Put that way, there's no excuse for constituents not to contribute. The Board welcomes everyone's participation.

The FASB Report No. 254
March 31, 2004
Pages 2 - 3

FASB's Outreach to a Vast Network of Constituents

The FASB has broad outreach to its constituents that helps strengthen its process. The Board maintains a network of over 250 constituents that actively participate in the development of its standards. The network includes the following groups and organizations:

- Financial Accounting Standards Advisory Council
- User Advisory Council
- Small Business Advisory Committee
- Project Resource Groups
    - Business Combinations
    - Equity-Based Compensation
    - Valuation Resource Group
    - Financial Instruments
    - Reporting Financial Performance
    - Revenue Recognition
    - Liability Extinguishment
    - Liability Equity
- 20+ liaison groups, representing various industries

The input received from constituents provides the FASB with a rich set of perspectives and experiences that are reflected in the Board's work.

Questions for Consideration

1. What point is the author trying to make in the article? Discuss.

2. Assume that the FASB is currently working on a standard for revenue recognition, i.e., when should revenue from the sale of its product be recorded in the company's books. As the FASB deliberates the new revenue recognition standard, what questions might a corporate manager pose to the FASB?

Assignment 4
The Income Statement, Balance Sheet and Statement of Stockholders' Equity

Name of your company _____

This assignment will analyze three of the four primary financial statements:

1. The *income statement* reports on the results of a company's operations.

2. The *balance sheet* gives the financial position of a company at the end of an accounting period.

3. The *statement of stockholders' equity* reports the results of all transactions that affect stockholder equity accounts.

4. The fourth statement, *statement of cash flows*, will be covered in Assignment 5.

There is no one approach to preparing financial statements. As you review the statements for your company, you will notice that all items referred to in the following sections may not be in your company's financial statements.

Often, the financial statement will have the word "consolidated" in its title to indicate that the corporation owns one or more subsidiaries and that the financial results of the subsidiaries have been combined with those of the parent company to produce a single set of financial statements.

Completing the Assignment

1. Consolidation

    a. Does your firm prepare consolidated financial statements?

      _____ Yes   _____ No   (If no, ignore part b.)

    b. When the company and the subsidiaries are combined, all transactions between the company and its subsidiaries must first be eliminated. Why do you think this is necessary?

    _____

    _____

    _____

    _____

2. The Income Statement

    a. What format was used to prepare your firm's income statement? (Check one.)

      _____ Single-step

      _____ Multiple-step

      Hint: *If gross margin (also called gross profit) is reported on the income statement, it's the multiple-step format. Otherwise, the single-step format has been used.*

    b. What is your company's total sales revenue?

Most recent year	Next most recent year	Percent change (use – for negative change)
$ _____	$ _____	_____ %

> **Note**
> To better compare one year to the next or one firm to another, a company often prepares *common size financial statements*, which relate line items on a financial statement relative to one specific item, e.g., sales or revenue for the income statement, and total assets for the balance sheet.

    c. For each of the selected items on the income statement, determine its percentage relative to sales or revenue for the most recent year and the next most recent year. If not reported by your company, draw a line through it.

Income Statement Line	Most recent year	Percent of sales	Next most recent year	Percent of sales
Sales or revenue	$ _____	_____ %	$ _____	_____ %
Cost of sales	_____	_____	_____	_____
Gross profit/margin	_____	_____	_____	_____
Operating expenses	_____	_____	_____	_____
Income before tax	_____	_____	_____	_____
Provision for tax	_____	_____	_____	_____
Net income	_____	_____	_____	_____
Other major items:				
_____	_____	_____	_____	_____
_____	_____	_____	_____	_____

    d. Based on the above common size analysis, which item(s) appear to be the most significant in explaining the change in net income (profitability) from the next most recent year to the most recent year, i.e., which items changed the most relative to the year's sales revenue? Briefly discuss.

_____

_____

_____

_____

_____

_____

e. Determine whether either of the following "special items" appear on the most recent income statement, usually near the end. Indicate whether the item appears and (if it appears) whether it increased or decreased net income. Explain the underlying event or transaction that caused the item to arise.

Hint: *Rarely will a company have more than one of these special items.*

	Item present?	Increased	Decreased
Discontinued operations	_____	_____	_____

_____

_____

_____

Extraordinary gain (or loss)	_____	_____	_____

_____

_____

_____

f. Using your judgment, list the *major* items of revenue and expense that are reported on your company's most recent income statement. For each item, indicate whether it is a revenue or an expense. Do not include any of the special items from Part e. above.

	Revenue	Expense
_____	_____	_____
_____	_____	_____
_____	_____	_____
_____	_____	_____
_____	_____	_____

3. The Balance Sheet

a. Which of the following terms describes the balance sheet as reported by your firm? (Check those that apply.)

_____   Classified balance sheet (i.e., assets are segregated into categories)

_____   Comparative balance sheet (i.e., more than one year of data is presented)

b. All publicly held companies are required to prepare a comparative three-year income statement and two-year balance sheet. Why are comparative financial statements required?

_____

_____

_____

c. If your company presented a classified balance sheet, identify the amounts your firm reported for each of the following categories and the percentage of *total assets* that each represents.

Hint: *All long-term liabilities are those amounts not classified as current.*

	Amount	Percent
Current assets	$_____	_____
Property, plant, and equipment	$_____	_____
Goodwill and other intangible assets	$_____	_____
Other long-term assets	$_____	_____
Total	$_____	100%
Current liabilities	$_____	_____
Long-term liabilities	$_____	_____
Contributed capital	$_____	_____
Retained earnings	$_____	_____
Total	$_____	100%

> **Note**
> If you were a creditor of a firm (i.e., the firm owed you money), you would be interested in whether the firm had enough resources to pay you when your bill came due, which can be determined by two indicators:
>
> 1. the amount of working capital (sometimes called net working capital), and
>
> (continued on the next page)

32

2. the current ratio (sometimes called the working capital ratio).

   Working capital (WC) is the cushion by which total current assets exceed total current liabilities.

   $$WC \; = \; \text{current assets - current liabilities}$$

   The current ratio (CR) reveals how many dollars of current assets are available to pay off each dollar of current liabilities.

   $$CR \; = \; \frac{\text{current assets}}{\text{current liabilities}}$$

d. What amount of working capital did your company have as of the date of its two most recent balance sheets? What was the current ratio, also known as the working capital ratio, at the end of the two most recent years?

   Important: *If your firm didn't prepare a classified balance sheet, you can't compute the amount of working capital and the current ratio. If that's the case, skip to f on the next page.*

	Most Recent Balance Sheet	**Next Most Recent Balance Sheet**
Working capital	$ _____	$ _____
Working capital ratio	_____ %	_____ %

e. For comparison to other firms, check with five classmates (who are analyzing different firms) to see what their working capital results were. Record those results below along with those of your firm. List the names of each comparative firm.

   Alternative: As an alternative to comparing your company to those of your classmates, you may want to use four or five other companies' financial statements that you get from the Internet. These companies can be used in later assignments, and can be from either your industry or different industries. Check with your professor to make sure this alternative is acceptable.

	Most Recent Year	**Next Most Recent Year**
Your firm _____	_____ %	_____ %
_____	_____	_____
_____	_____	_____
_____	_____	_____
_____	_____	_____
_____	_____	_____

f.   How does your firm appear to compare to the other firms you listed above regarding its ability to pay current liabilities as they become due?

_____

_____

_____

_____

_____

Note on Ratio Analysis

Several techniques are available to analyze a company's financial health. A common method is to calculate ratios and compare them with industry norms and/or the company over time. There are three common ratios that use information found on the *income statement* and *balance sheet* that allow users to assess the overall profitability of a company. The financial statements provide most of the data needed to calculate most ratios.

1. *profit margin* assesses the relationship between a company's sales and net income;

2. *return on assets* measures the ability of the company to generate profit from its investment in assets; and

3. *return on equity* measures the return (income) on stockholders' (common) equity.

Another calculation commonly made to analyze profitability is to determine the change in net income from one year to the next.

---

g.   Compute your company's *profit margin*.

$$\text{Profit margin} = \frac{\text{Net income}}{\text{Sales}}$$

Current year	Next most recent year
_____%	_____%

What does this ratio indicate about your company's ability to convert sales into profit? Discuss.

_____

_____

_____

_____

_____

_____

h. Compute your company's *return on asset* ratio.

$$\text{Return on assets} = \frac{\text{Net income}}{\text{Total assets}}$$

**Current
  year**

**Next most
recent year**

_____%   _____%

What does this ratio indicate about your company's using its assets profitably? Discuss.

_____

_____

_____

_____

_____

i. Calculate your company's *return on equity* ratio.

$$\text{Return on equity} = \frac{\text{Net income}}{\text{Total stockholders' equity}}$$

**Current
  year**

**Next most
recent year**

_____%   _____%

What does this ratio indicate about how well your company has performed for its stockholders? Discuss.

_____

_____

_____

_____

_____

4. The Statement of Stockholders' Equity

   a. Did your company include a statement of stockholders' equity with the rest of its financial statements? (Check one.)

      _____ Yes   _____ No   (If no, ignore part b.)

   b. Carefully review the most recent year's data on the statement of stockholders' equity. Were there any significant changes between the beginning of the year and the end of the most recent year? If so, complete the table below for the significant changes. In the change column, use parentheses to indicate a balance that decreased.

      Ignore changes that you judge to be insignificant. If your company had no significant changes in the amounts comprising stockholders' equity, note that on the first line.

Statement of Stockholders' Equity Accounts	Balance at Beginning of Year	Balance at End of Year	Change in Balance During Year
_____	$ _____	$ _____	$ _____
_____	_____	_____	_____
_____	_____	_____	_____
_____	_____	_____	_____
_____	_____	_____	_____
_____	_____	_____	_____

5. Articulation of Financial Statements

   Articulation of Financial Statements refers to information on one financial statement being related to information on another financial statement. For instance, the year-end balance of common stock appears in both the balance sheet and statement of stockholders' equity. Find another example of articulation in your company's financial statements. Describe it.

   _____

   _____

   _____

   _____

   _____

Reading 4
Widening the Gap: Big GAAP vs. Little GAAP

Reprinted with permission from *Financial Executive*.

By Colleen Sayther

President's Page

Half of the United States' economic output is driven by nonpublic entities. There are more than 22 million private businesses in the U.S., and approximately 17,000 public companies. Every so often, the debate arises as to whether separate accounting and reporting standards should be set for small and medium-sized enterprises (SMEs).

This time, it seems to be gaining momentum as recent trends in standard-setting have increased the differences between the needs of users of financial statements. Many small companies feel that as the Financial Accounting Standards Board (FASB)'s rulemaking has become more complex, they simply don't have the wherewithal to keep up, particularly as they look at some of the far-reaching projects on FASB's agenda, such as the evident move towards fair value accounting. (Truth be told, many large companies feel the same way!)

To limit compliance costs, some companies chose to depart from certain GAAP requirements and to have qualified audit or review reports, or moved from audited or reviewed statements to compilation engagements. Several factors have influenced this renewed interest and momentum in developing separate standards for SMEs:

■ The IASB issued "Preliminary Views on Accounting Standards for Small and Medium-sized Entities" in June ("the PV"). The PV reacts to concerns from countries that have chosen to adopt the International Financial Reporting Standards (IFRS) that SMEs need to be separately addressed. Since many of these countries already have differential standards for SMEs, the alternative is to have separate SME accounting standards, inconsistent with IFRS, that are set by individual country accounting standard-setters. Many believe that this is an inefficient way to set such standards.

■ Many other countries, including Canada in 2002, already have established differential GAAP for SMEs.

■ The Sarbanes-Oxley Act of 2002 mandates that funding for the FASB, as well as the Public Company Accounting Oversight Board (PCAOB), come from public companies only.

■ The needs of financial statements users are different for nonpublic entities and public entities.

Another issue is that FASB is now funded by public companies only. Formerly, funding came from a variety of sources, including accounting firms, investment companies, trade associations and nonpublic companies. The change has many SMEs concerned that FASB standard-setting will be principally focused on those companies from which its funding comes. This argument has also been used for auditing standards, since the PCAOB is focused on firms that audit SEC registrants.

For its part, FASB recently established the Small Business Advisory Committee to ensure that as it moves forward with future rulemaking, the concerns of private and small public companies are being heard. We were asked to nominate potential members, and, as a result, several FEI members are participating.

In existing GAAP there have been instances where exemptions for small or nonpublic businesses have been made, as well as instances where nonpublic companies or companies under a certain size have been afforded longer adoption times. Additionally, the American Institute of Certified Public Accountants (AICPA) has also set up a task force to study this issue. FEI is participating on this task force as well.

As we think about differential accounting standards, there are obviously many issues to consider: Would this cause more investor confusion? What happens to the comparability of private and public companies, and between U.S. and offshore companies? What happens when a private company goes public? Will investors and other users of information respect one kind of accounting more than the other? Are there really two correct ways to account for transactions?

Another issue is whether the content of financial statements should be driven by financial statement users' needs. Public company financial statements are widely circulated and available to an unlimited number of users, who benefit from access to a broad range of detailed financial information, making the

size of the company largely irrelevant. Or should an accounting transaction be accounted for and disclosed the same way, regardless of the entity? (If Joe's Lemonade Stand enters into complex derivatives, shouldn't it account for them as a large company does?)

Creating differential standards would also take a great deal of coordination among the regulatory bodies, preparers, auditors and users of financial statements. Some users of financial reports have expressed concerns that a "big GAAP/little GAAP" system could undermine

the comparability and credibility of financial reports. They believe that such a two tiered system also would add costs to the users, auditors and preparers that would likely more than offset any perceived benefits. It is clear that many issues need to be discussed and resolved before this becomes a reality in the U.S. I encourage you to get involved in the debate.

Financial Executive
September 2004
Page 6

Questions for Consideration

1. Several factors are listed supporting and others opposing differential GAAP for large and small companies. List the three factors supporting and three opposing differential GAAP that you believe are the most significant.

2. Do you believe that a transaction should be recognized, measured, and disclosed differently because of the size of the company? Explain.

Assignment 5
Statement of Cash Flows

Assignment 4 highlighted the basic elements of the balance sheet, income statement, and statement of stockholders' equity. The statement of cash flows is the fourth basic financial statement. Many believe that it may be the most important because it explains the sources and uses of cash—the life blood of a corporation.

The statement of cash flows is divided into three sections:
- cash flow from operating activities;
- cash flow from investing activities; and
- cash flow from financing activities.

Each section details the flow of cash into and out of the company's three major activities.

The purpose of this Assignment is to study the basics of the statement of cash flows.

Completing the Assignment

1. Which format does your company use to report the statement of cash flows? (Check one.)

   _____ Direct format   The section on operating activities begins with a direct format line such as "Cash received from customers."

   _____ Indirect format   The section on operating activities begins with a line such as "Net income" or "Net loss" and then proceeds to add and subtract items from that amount.

2. In the spaces following, fill in the proper summary amounts from your company's most recent statement of cash flows. If any of the three categories represent a net cash outflow, show that amount in parentheses.

   a. Net cash inflow (outflow) from *operating* activities $ _____

   b. Net cash inflow (outflow) from *investing* activities $ _____

      List the two largest transactions

      _____

      _____

   c. Net cash inflow (outflow) from *financing* activities $ _____

List the two largest transactions

_____

_____

    d. Net increase (decrease) in cash, or sometimes labeled
       net change in cash and cash equivalents, for the year $ _____

3. Now go back to the balance sheet and fill in the following amounts that are reported for Cash (under the assets category).

    a. Current year's ending cash balance $ _____

    b. Prior year's ending cash balance $ _____

    c. Change in cash balance during the current year $ _____

    d. Does the number on line 3.c) above match the number on line 2.d) above? (check one)

      _____ Yes   _____ No

    Hint: *They should match. This is an example of financial statement* articula-tion, *which means that numbers reported on one financial statement are related to numbers on the other statements, referred to in Assignment 4.*

    If the amounts do not match, by how much do they differ?

    _____

Interpreting the Statement of Cash Flows

4. Compare the amounts for Net Income and Cash Flow from Operations.

    a. Are they the same amount?   _____ Yes   _____ No

    b. By how much do they differ? $ _____

    c. What appears to be the largest cause for the difference?

    _____

    _____

    _____

5. Based on the information in the statement of cash flows, determine the amount of cash sales for the most recent year.

    $ _____

6. Is your company's cash flow from operations sufficient to cover its acquisitions of operating assets (e.g., property, plant and equipment)?

    _____ Yes   _____ No

7. Discuss the significance of the relationship between cash flow from operations and acquisition of operating assets (investing activities).

    _____

    _____

    _____

    _____

    _____

Note

Recently, two new measures have gained popularity as management tries to improve the appearance of earnings. They attempt to restate reported net income to an amount similar to cash flow from operations. Specifically, the two measures are:

▸   EBIT (earnings before interest and tax); and

▸   EBITDA (earnings before interest, tax, depreciation and amortization).

---

8. Calculate EBIT for your company.

    Net income $ _____

    Interest expense   _____

    Tax   _____

    EBIT $ _____

9. Calculate EBITDA for your company.

    Net income $ _____

    Interest expense   _____

    Taxes   _____

    Depreciation   _____   (Depreciation and amortiza-

    Amortization   _____   tion are often combined.)

    EBITDA $ _____

(This assignment continues on the next page.)

10. Enter net income, cash flow from operations, EBIT and EBITDA. State which amount you believe is the best representation of your company's operations? Explain.

   $ _____   Net income

   $ _____   Cash flow from operations

   $ _____   EBIT

   $ _____   EBITDA

   _____

   _____

   _____

   _____

   _____

   _____

   _____

   _____

Reading 5
Where's the Cash?

Reprinted by permission of *Forbes Magazine* ©2004 Forbes Inc.

By Steve Hanke
Professor of Applied Economics at The John Hopkins University and a Senior Fellow at the Cato Institute

Point of View

"Earnings are opinion; cash is a fact." First recorded in the 1890s, that adage deserves to be etched in bronze above every investor's desk. And we're talking not just about net earnings but also about all the modern variations on that figure, such as operating earnings, a.k.a. Ebitda (earnings before interest, taxes, depreciation and amortization). You might think that by focusing on operating earnings, as leveraged-buyout meisters are wont to do, you avoid one of the most subjective aspects of net income, namely the rate at which capital expenditures are charged off to earnings as depreciation. But, as Warren Buffett has wisely noted, Ebitda can be even more dangerous than net income because it tempts the investor to think of cap-ex as a luxury.

"Among those who talk about Ebitda and those who don't, there are more frauds among those who do," Buffett once said. "Either they are trying to con you, or they're conning themselves." In the 2003 annual report for Berkshire Hathaway, Buffett defines intrinsic value as "the discounted value of the cash that can be taken out of a business during its remaining life." Note the word "cash." That would be cash after necessary levels of capital outlays. If you want to know what FedEx is worth, look at what's left after it has paid for trucks and airplanes, not before.

Why isn't the bottom line a good measure of extractable cash? Because so many of the numbers above it in the profit-and-loss statement are subjective. Depreciation isn't the only fuzzy number. There are several ways to account for long-term contracts, in which payments can run ahead of or behind the work. How should a fluctuating derivative contract be evaluated on the books? In liquid markets you can mark it to recent market value. In illiquid ones you have to "guess." What is the true cost of your workers' pensions? A myriad of actuarial and investment judgments determine the answer to that question. The valuation of foreign assets involves assumptions about exchange rates. The treatment of stock options can give the best accountants a headache. Goodwill is yet another accounting issue subject to widely varying opinion. Impairment of long-lived assets involves write-downs, but when? Yet another judgment call.

What's interesting about all these choices is that not a single one changes the balance in the company's checking account. If you want a fair measure of extractable cash, the ultimate end in running a business, try free cash flow. To get the number, start with "cash flow from operations" shown on the flow-of-funds page right after the P&L. Now subtract maintenance-level cap-ex. Absent any clear-cut information about which plant and equipment outlays expanded the business and which merely kept existing business alive, assume that all fell into the latter category.

This little exercise won't guarantee that you will fill your portfolio with the next Microsoft, but it might save you from investing in a WorldCom. Take a look at the chart [next page], which displays Ebitda and free cash flow for the now-bankrupt telecom (which has since changed its name to MCI). We measure from 1996 through 2001; the company declared bankruptcy in mid-2002. WorldCom was reporting terrific earnings, but it was somehow always tapped out. Unless you had subpoena power, you couldn't have determined what was going on—the company was doctoring its P&L by recording ongoing access-fee payments as capital outlays. But by looking at free cash flow, you might have been suspicious. Buffett wouldn't have touched this outfit with a barge pole.

A similar exercise with Adelphia Communications shows Ebitda zooming from

$206 million to $1,084 million between March 1996 and December 2000 (date of the last SEC 10-K filing) while free cash flow collapsed from a negative $36 million to a negative $1,649 million. Bid up to $74 a share in January 2000, this is another company now keeping bankruptcy lawyers busy.

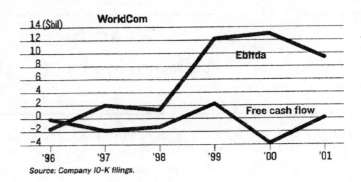

Source: Company 10-K filings.

Forbes
April 12, 2004
Page 230

Questions for Consideration

1. What amounts on the income statement are considered subjective, or fuzzy, and what is their effect on net income and cash flow? Explain.

2. Why would an analysis of free cash flow have indicated WorldCom's cash flow problems? Explain.

Name _____ Professor _____

Course _____ Section _____

Assignment 6
The SEC Form10-K and Proxy Statement

Name of your company: _____

The Securities and Exchange Commission (SEC), an agency of the federal government, was established by the Securities Exchange Act of 1934. Its primary function is to promote full-disclosure of all pertinent financial material and other information concerning securities offered for public sale. The SEC does not prevent the sale of risky or low-quality securities, but strives to make sure that investors are fully informed as to the nature of the investment they are making.

The purpose of this assignment is for you to understand the similarities and differences between a company's Annual Report to Shareholders and its SEC Form 10-K, which must be submitted to the SEC annually. In addition, you will review interesting information in your firm's proxy statement.

In general, companies are subject to SEC regulation if they have:
- assets of $1 million or more;
- 500 or more stockholders; or
- their securities (e.g., stocks or bonds) are traded publicly.

Principal among SEC regulations is the filing of regular public reports with the Commission. While there are more than a dozen different reporting forms used by SEC registrants, the three most commonly used reporting documents are the following SEC forms.
- 10-Q – the quarterly report to the SEC
- 8-K – an as-needed report of unscheduled events or corporate changes important to shareholders or the SEC. For example, when a company changes independent auditors it must announce that event by filing an 8-K with the SEC.
- 10-K – the annual report to the SEC

The 10-K is, by far, the best known of the SEC-required reports. In essence, it is a special version of the company's Annual Report.

> ## On the Internet
> Since 1996 the SEC has required all public companies to make their required SEC filings (e.g., 10-Qs, 8-Ks, 10-Ks) electronically. These filings are then posted to the SEC's web site within 24 hours. This system is called EDGAR, which stands for Electronic Data Gathering, Analysis, and Retrieval.

If you have not secured a copy of your company's 10-K and proxy statement, you can download a copy from EDGAR at **www.sec.gov**. At the home page click on "Search for Company Filings" and then "Companies and Other Filers." Enter your company's information.

Completing the Assignment

1. The SEC 10-K Report is comprised of 15 items organized into four parts. Review your company's 10-K and note the page(s) where each item is reported.

Page(s) Where Item is Reported

Part I

Item 1.   Business   _____

Item 2.   Properties   _____

Item 3.   Legal Proceedings   _____

Item 4.   Submission of Matters to Vote of Security Holders   _____

Part II

Item 5.   Market for the Registrant's Common Equity, Related Stockholder Matters, and Issuer Purchases of Equity Securities   _____

Item 6.   Selected Financial Data   _____

Item 7.   Management's Discussion and Analysis of Financial Condition and Results of Operations   _____

Item 7A.   Quantitative and Qualitative Disclosures About Market Risk   _____

Item 8.   Financial Statements and Supplementary Data   _____

Item 9.   Changes in and Disagreements with Accountants on Accounting and Financial Disclosure   _____

Item 9A.   Controls and Procedures   _____

Item 9B.   Other Information   _____

Part III

Item 10.   Directors and Executive Officers of the Registrant   _____

Item 11.   Executive Compensation   _____

Item 12.   Security Ownership of Certain Beneficial Owners and Management and Related Stockholder Matters   _____

Item 13.   Certain Relationships and Related Transactions   _____

Item 14.   Principal Accountant Fees and Services   _____

Part IV

Item 15.   Exhibits and Financial Statement Schedules   _____

2. Compare your firm's annual report to its SEC Form 10-K and answer the following. *(A few companies combine their annual report and SEC Form 10-K. If your company has combined the two reports, skip to question 3.)*

   a. Indicate with a check (✓) where the item appears.

Selected Information Item	Appears in Annual report	Appears in SEC 10-K
Audit report	_____	_____
Balance Sheet	_____	_____
Business property (detailed)	_____	_____
Footnotes to financial statements	_____	_____
Income Statement	_____	_____
Letter to shareholders	_____	_____
Management discussion and analysis (MD&A)	_____	_____
Pictures of products and/or employees	_____	_____
Report of Management Responsibilities	_____	_____
Segment information	_____	_____
Signatures	_____	_____
Statement of Cash Flows	_____	_____
Statement of Stockholders' Equity	_____	_____
Other significant items:		
_____	_____	_____
_____	_____	_____

   b. As evident from 2.a. above, not all information items appear in both the annual report and SEC Form 10K. Explain why you think this happens.

_____

_____

_____

_____

_____

_____

_____

_____

3. Answer the following based on information disclosed in your company's proxy statement.

 a. What is the date and location of the stockholders' meeting?

  Date _____

  Location _____

 b. To be eligible to vote, a shareholder must be a shareholder on the date of record. What is your company's date of record? _____

 c. How many members of the Board of Directors are to be elected? _____

 d. How many proposals are advanced by management for action? _____

 e. Briefly describe one or two proposals, issues, or topics submitted for vote by management.

  1) _____

  _____

  _____

  2) _____

  _____

  _____

 f. How many proposals, if any, are to be acted upon that are advanced by stockholders? _____

 g. Briefly describe one or two proposals, issues, or topics, if any, submitted for vote by stockholders.

  1) _____

  _____

  _____

  2) _____

  _____

  _____

 h. Find a section detailing the fees paid to the independent auditors and fill in the blanks below.

  $ _____ for audit fees

  $ _____ for audit related fees

  $ _____ for tax fees

  $ _____ for other fees

  $ _____ total of independent auditor's fees

 i. Is there a section discussing the executive compensation from the company's Compensation Committee? _____ Yes _____ No

j. For your firm's highest paid executive, compute the total dollar amount of compensation (e.g., salary + bonus + etc.) that he/she received from the company in each of the last three years.

For perspective about how your firm's highest paid executive compares to those of other firms, check with five classmates (who are studying different firms) and record their information in thousands of dollars (000's).

Alternative

As an alternative to comparing your company's highest paid executive to those of your classmates' companies, you may want to compare with the companies you used in No. 3.e. of Assignment 4.

Check with your professor to make sure this option is acceptable.

Highest Paid Executive's Total Compensation	Your Firm	COMPARATIVE FIRMS				
		Firm 1	Firm 2	Firm 3	Firm 4	Firm 5
Most recent year	_____	_____	_____	_____	_____	_____
Next most recent year	_____	_____	_____	_____	_____	_____
Next most recent year	_____	_____	_____	_____	_____	_____

k. How does the total compensation of your firm's highest-paid executive compare to the highest-paid executives of your comparative firms over the past three years? Discuss.

_____

_____

_____

_____

_____

_____

_____

l. Inspect the stock performance graph usually found near the end of the proxy statement. How does your company's price performance compare to that of its peer group? Briefly discuss.

_____

_____

_____

_____

_____

How does your company's price performance compare to that of an S & P index (normally, S & P 500)? Briefly discuss.

_____

_____

_____

_____

Does the trend in stock returns match the trend in compensation being paid to the company's top executive? Discuss.

_____

_____

_____

_____

4. Optional Memo No. 2 – Company disclosure

One of the primary ways by which a company informs the public about its financial status is through its annual report and SEC filings. Write a memo based on these financial reports.

Guide for Memo No. 2

a. Does your company's overall disclosure system—its annual report and SEC filings (10-K and proxy)—appear to contain sufficient information to give you a working knowledge about your company's financial status? Explain.

b. Based on your analysis of your company so far, would you recommend that an investor acquire stock in your company? Why or why not?

Reading 6
A Matter of Emphasis

By Alix Nyberg

Regulation G was supposed to end the abuses of pro forma reporting. Has it succeeded?

When the Securities and Exchange Commission issued Regulation G in January 2003, some people thought the death knell had been sounded for the abuse of pro forma numbers.

From that date on, any non-GAAP number used in an earnings release had to be accompanied by—and reconciled to—the "most directly comparable" GAAP number. Anything excluded from the pro forma metric had to be disclosed. At the same time, the SEC also amended existing rules to narrow the field of what could be excluded from pro forma measures in filed information.

Today, though, there's little evidence that Reg G has had much effect on pro forma reporting. About 60 percent of companies continued to report non-GAAP information in their first-quarter earnings releases this year, according to a National Investor Relations Institute (NIRI) survey of 360 companies, down from the 70 percent that reported doing so in the quarter before Reg G took effect. Of those that stopped using pro forma, only about a quarter attributed the move to Reg G.

Some observers, in fact, charge that abuses of pro forma still flourish. "There seem to be a lot of companies that are pushing the envelope on Reg G," says Chuck Hill, former director of research at Thomson Financial First Call. While few are blatantly breaking the law by omitting GAAP equivalents or reconciliation tables, Hill says some companies are taking advantage of the relatively lax enforcement of regulations on press releases to spin their numbers in ways that would be illegal in official filings.

Consider Intuit, a Mountain View, California-based provider of business and financial software. Pro forma earnings have actually moved higher up in the company's earnings releases since Reg G took effect, with this years third-quarter release (dated May 19) headlining a 14 percent growth in pro forma earnings per share. GAAP EPS, which was higher in absolute terms but reflected a decline from last year's numbers, shows up immediately below, halfway down the page. And the difference between the two is explained only in general terms in a footnote to the release, with details following in a separate file.

Such placement, charges Hill, may not be a technical violation, but it "is definitely a violation of the spirit of the law" requiring that GAAP numbers get equal or greater prominence than pro forma. He adds that "everybody ought to at least start in the same place—GAAP—before moving into adjustments."

Intuit is hardly alone; a host of other companies, particularly software and biotech firms, continue to give pro forma first place, according to Hill (see "Pro Pro Forma," page 53). But they do so at their own peril, in view of what many securities lawyers advise. "Given that the SEC says non-GAAP financial measures can lend themselves to being misleading, its important to put them in context," says Katharine Martin of Wilson Sonsini Goodrich & Rosati. "I would personally not recommend that you use non-GAAP financial measures in the lead, because there's a chance that it could get more prominence, particularly in wire stories."

A RECURRING ISSUE

Companies that routinely exclude recurring items, such as restructuring charges, from pro forma calculations are also coming in for criticism. "You still see items like restructuring charges going in, and you look at the reconciliation tables and you've got [charges] across all years," says Lynn Turner, former SEC chief accountant and now principal with San Francisco-based Glass, Lewis & Co. "Investors need to realize these really are recurring charges."

Again, the practice is not a technical violation of Reg G. Companies can adjust earnings for recurring items in their press releases, according to SEC spokesman John Heine, so long as they provide a chart reconciling the adjusted numbers to GAAP with the release. (Such adjustments to GAAP are only prohibited in a company's 10-Ks and 10-Qs, which are covered by an amendment to regulations S-K and S-B that was written concurrently with Reg G.)

However, the SEC continues to have wide latitude on what it considers misleading. Beginning an earnings release with pro forma results and burying GAAP numbers, for example, "of course would be a violation of Reg G," according to one SEC official. "Even before Reg G, we brought a case on that issue," referring to the 2002 cease-and-desist order levied against Trump Hotels & Casino Resorts Inc. for touting a pro forma profit without revealing that it excluded one-time charges but not one-time gains until it made an official filing with the SEC.

With no SEC enforcement actions on Reg G to date, attorneys say the agency has so far been sympathetic to the complexities of the law, which imposes detailed requirements such as posting reconciliation tables on the corporate Website for any non-GAAP measures used in an earnings call and giving the Website address to analysts before a presentation. "I think the SEC staff understands this is complicated," says Martin, and generally gives companies in

violation a chance to fix the problem before imposing penalties. However, the agency "is definitely looking at Reg G compliance as part of its periodic reviews."

To be sure, some companies have dropped non-GAAP measures altogether. But going cold turkey has its disadvantages as well. Louis M. Thompson, NIRI's president and CEO, points out that most analysts continue to make estimates on a non-GAAP basis. As a result, "some of the companies that go to GAAP-only find themselves penalized by the market when they come in lower than First Call mean [estimates]," making it seem like they missed their numbers.

AVOIDING CONFUSION

To prevent such misunderstandings, Wellesley, Massachusetts-based PerkinElmer Inc. began including First Call estimates in its earnings releases last fall, making reference to the estimate in the opening of the release and providing it as a line item in its non-GAAP-to-GAAP reconciliation tables. "When the media spit out PerkinElmer misses because they were confused, we had to do something," says company spokesman Dan Sutherby.

And many point out that pro forma numbers are still perfectly defensible, if used for the right reasons. In fact, John Kenny, CFO of Boston-based document-management firm Iron Mountain Inc., says it was at the SECs request that the firm began to use the term "Adjusted EBITDA" for its primary earnings metric three years ago. After a routine review of the highly

leveraged firm's filings, says Kenny, the SEC asked Iron Mountain to publish the adjusted form so that investors could better track the firm's performance against its bond covenants using that metric.

When Reg G emerged, however, Iron Mountain's adjusted measure suddenly became unusable, thanks to the new S-K/S-B amendment stipulating that neither GAAP nor pro forma results in filings may exclude items if similar ones have been excluded in the previous two years, or are expected to be excluded within the following two years. "The problem with Adjusted EBITDA was that some of the things we were adjusting out—the foreign-exchange gains and losses, some merger-related costs, and costs associated with refinancing— were occurring on a fairly regular basis," says Kenny.

As a result, the company dropped Adjusted EBITDA and introduced operating income before depreciation and amortization (OIBDA) in both its releases and its filings. This measure does not exclude any recurring charges, Kenny says, and is easier to reconcile to GAAP net income.

Given what seems to be a more judicious use of pro forma numbers—the spread between GAAP and operating earnings for the S&P 500 narrowed to 11 percent for 2003 and dropped to 4 percent in the first quarter of 2004—and the rigorous disclosure that accompanies them, at least one longtime critic of pro forma is happy with the changes Reg G has sparked. "What we do have today is absolutely better than what we had before the regulation," says Turner, who dubbed pro forma earnings as "everything but the bad stuff" during his tenure at the SEC. "Now at least people are getting reconciliations to GAAP, and they're doing things consistently."

CFO
July 2004
Pages 69 - 70

Pro Pro Forma

Some S&P 500 companies that continue to give prominence to pro forma.

Company • Details for Most Recent Quarterly Release

BMC Software • Net earnings excluding special items ($40.8 million) leads the April 29 release, and is the basis for the company's forward guidance, GAAP earnings of $36.9 million come later in the first paragraph, with the difference explained only in an attached table.

Chiron • Headlines pro forma earnings of 22 cents per share, the 14 cents GAAP earnings show up later in the body of the April 21 release. Despite a lengthy discussion of the rationale for pro forma, the details of what is excluded are left to the attached table.

Hewlett-Packard • Puts $1.3 billion non-GAAP operating profit ahead of $1.1 billion GAAP in the May 18 release, but notes that both include a one-time legal settlement and follows with EPS based on net income. Guidance given on non-GAAP-basis only.

PeopleSoft • Pro forma net income of $62 million comes in the second paragraph of its April 29 release, with GAAP net income of $24 million following it, noting that the difference is partially due to purchase accounting adjustments for its J.D. Edwards acquisition. The two are reconciled in a table in the text.

Sabre Holdings • Adjusted EPS of 37 cents and GAAP EPS of 31 cents both get a headline, but the difference between the two is relegated to page 8 of the April 22 release.

Sanmina • While noting in the first paragraph that the reconciliations from GAAP to pro forma are attached, Sanmina gives the 5 cents per share pro forma gain a bullet point at the top of its April 20 release, while confining the 9 cents GAAP loss to a table that follows pro forma results in the text. Guidance given on a pro forma basis only.

Sources: Chuck Hill/Thomson Financial First Call; company Websites

---

Questions for Consideration

1. Discuss briefly why it was necessary for the SEC to issue Regulation G.

2. Assume that Tellall Co. had restructuring charges of $50,000 and an Environmental Protection Agency fine of $33,000, which were both omitted from calculating its pro forma earnings of $80,000. Prepare a reconciliation schedule from pro forma earnings to GAAP earnings. Comment on the difference.

Assignment 7
Initial Report about Your Company

As described in Chapter F6 of the Ingram, et al, text, the development of financial accounting reports has evolved over time. Prior to the Securities Acts of 1933 and 1934, financial statements of many companies had limited disclosures and were, at times, fraudulent or misleading. Since then publically traded companies are required to adhere to accounting and reporting standards that have been established by both the public sector, i.e., the Securities and Exchange Commission, and the private sector, i.e., the Financial Accounting Standards Board.

Even today, however, there may be times when financial reporting fails to provide transparent financial statements which clearly report on all of a company's activities. Though many believe that U.S. financial reporting is the best in the world, many also contend that more transparent financial statements may have averted the fall of such firms as Enron and WorldCom.

Though you have not studied in detail the accounting complexities of many individual financial statement accounts (such as depreciation methods and cost flow techniques, which will be studied in the remainder of the ARP assignments), you should have gained an overall understanding of the financial statements and the company's SEC Form 10-K and proxy statement.

Specifically, you should know:

- about your company and its industry,
- basic environmental factors affecting your company,
- required SEC Form 10-K and proxy disclosures, and
- essential information found in the income statement, balance sheet, statement of stockholders' equity, and statement of cash flows.

Completing the Assignment

Your professor may require you to prepare a formal written report about your company which could include the following.

1. Your *initial reaction*, i.e., favorable or unfavorable, about your company. In your analysis you may want to consider the following:

   a. your company's industry;

   b. its major products or services;

   c. general economic and political environment;

    d. your company's position in the industry, i.e., does it appear to be a leader (pro-active) or follower (reactionary); and

    e. assessment of the non-financial information contained in your company's annual report.

2. The second part of your report should answer the following questions in one or two additional pages.

    a. Does your company's overall disclosure system—its annual report and SEC filings (10-K and proxy)—appear to contain sufficient information to give you a working knowledge about your company's financial status? Explain.

    b. Based on your analysis of your company so far, would you recommend that an investor acquire stock in your company? Why or why not?

Name _____   Professor _____

Course _____   Section _____

Assignment 8
Notes to the Financial Statements and the Time Value of Money

Name of your company _____

As stated in Assignment 3, notes to the financial statements are an important part of financial reporting and disclosure. They provide detail and further explanation for data reported on the face of the financial statements.

At the bottom of every audited set of financial statements, a sentence such as this is found: "The accompanying notes are an integral part of the financial statements," or "See the accompanying notes to the financial statements." This alerts the reader that important information is contained within the notes and that failure to read it may cause the financial statements to be misleading.

No two companies have exactly the same set of notes or even the same set of topics discussed therein. Conceivably, any line item on any of the financial statements could result in a note. Nevertheless, there are some observable patterns to the them.

The first note usually carries a title such as "Summary of Significant Accounting Policies." Under U.S. GAAP companies commonly have a choice of accounting method and the firm must report the choices it has made in this first note.

Other topics or issues that almost always result in a separate note are:
- inventories;
- long-term assets;
- long-term debt;
- income taxes;
- employee benefit plans (pensions);
- contingencies; and
- industry segments.

Interspersed among these listed items can be any number of other notes on other topics, including the time value of money as discussed in Chapter F8 of your text.

The purpose of this assignment is two-fold. The first purpose is to learn the types of information commonly disclosed in the notes to the financial statements. You will be asked to peruse them and to respond to certain questions about them. The second purpose is to use the notes to the financial statements to identify applications of the time value of money as discussed in Chapter F8 of your text.

Completing the Assignment

1. Locate the notes to the financial statements contained in your company's annual report. Scan them for the general topic that each covers and enter the appropriate information into Table A below.

Table A – Common Topics Covered by the Notes			
Is there a note about:	**No**	**Yes**	**If yes, Note #**
a. Significant accounting policies?			
Did a new financial accounting standard affect the financial statements during the current year?			
If yes, briefly explain the one with the greatest potential affect on the company's financial statements. _____ _____ _____			
b. Inventories?			
c. Long-term assets (deprecation)?			
d. Long-term debt?			
e. Income taxes?			
What is the effective tax rate? _____%			
f. Employee benefit plans (pensions)?			
If yes, what is the pension cost/(income) for the current year? $_____			
g. Contingencies (litigation)?			
h. Industry segments?			
If yes, how many segments are reported? _____			

2. The notes reviewed in Table A are just a few of the many notes accompanying the financial statements in an annual report. Select two other notes from your company's annual report that are *not* listed in Table A and complete Table B for each of the two notes.

Table B–Additional Topics Covered by the Notes	
Note #	**Subject Matter of Note**

3. Notes often reveal information that is based on (or related to) applications of the time value of money; information involving interest rates, risk, and time. Find the footnote about pensions (or post retirement benefits).

> **Note**
> An individual receives a pension in the future for work performed currently. Accrual accounting requires that the expense associated with the pension be recognized as the work is performed. Oversimplifying a complex calculation, pension expense for the current period is essentially the present value of the future cash payments. However, the interest rate used to discount the future payments is only an estimate. Changing the interest rate could affect the amount of pension expense.

a. Do the future pension payments represent a payment of a single amount or an annuity? _____

b. What assumed discount interest rate was used in the current period and prior period?

    _____ % current period   _____ % prior period

c. What affect would an *increase* in the discount rate have on pension expense for the period.

    Increase   Decrease   No effect   (Circle one)

    Why?_____

    _____

    _____

d. In the spaces provided, identify two notes and explain how you know that time value of money principles were involved (exclusive of pensions).

    Hint: *Present value applications usually are associated with long-term liabilities.*

Topic of note _____

Explanation _____

_____

_____

_____

_____

Topic of note _____

Explanation _____

_____

_____

_____

_____

e. Under what situation would your company apply the *future value* of a single
amount or an annuity concept?

_____

_____

_____

_____

_____

Reading 8
Auditors May Let Footnote Errors Slide

By Judith Burns

Location, a key factor in real estate, may be just as important in corporate accounting, according to a new study that finds auditors are more willing to tolerate errors when they appear in a footnote than in the main body of a financial report.

The report, released Friday by accounting professors at Cornell University, Ithaca, N.Y., and Bentley College, Waltham, Mass., casts doubt on the reliability of numbers tucked into footnotes to financial statements, including stock-option awards and some lease agreements.

In corporate financial results, information location influences reliability, the study found. It concluded that auditors are much more likely to demand companies correct misstatements involving stock options and leases when results are shown on the books than when they are disclosed elsewhere, such as in a footnote.

It's almost like flipping a switch on or off, said Mark Nelson, a professor at Cornell's Johnson Graduate School of Management.

Mr. Nelson and co-authors Robert Libby and James Hunton tested how experienced auditors at Big Four accounting firms reacted to errors in a public company's accounting.

In one experiment, auditors were asked how they would handle a company that had underestimated the cost of employee stock options, but objected to making any adjustment. Some auditors were told the firm included the cost of stock options on its income statement; others were told the cost was shown only in a footnote.

Even though the size of the error was the same in both cases, amounting to about 4.6% of net income, auditors had very different reactions. When the error was on the books, auditors called for a full or nearly full correction on average. When the error was in the footnote, the auditors rarely called for any correction.

Stock options give holders the right to buy or sell shares in the future at a preset price. Under a compromise adopted a decade ago, companies may show the fair value of option awards in a footnote or as an on-the-books business expense. That choice is set to end this summer when the Financial Accounting Standards Board will require firms to treat options as an expense.

In accounting, when an item such as stock options is controversial or hard to calculate, "What everybody always says is: Just put it in a footnote," Mr. Nelson said. He said the report might call that practice into question since it suggests numbers may be less reliable if you put them in the footnotes.

Researchers conducted a second experiment to see if auditors might have been swayed by the subjectivity involved in valuing stock options. They sought to remove that element by testing auditors' reaction to a company that didn't want to adjust an error that underestimated liability for leases by about 4.6% of total assets.

Accounting rules require companies to treat capital leases as an on-the-books expense, while allowing operating leases to remain off the books. Some companies voluntarily disclose liabilities implied by operating leases, and all companies provide enough information to estimate those liabilities.

Much like the stock-options experiment, faced with the same size error, auditors took a very different stance depending on whether the company's lease costs were on or off the books. On average, the study found auditors sought complete correction of errors of capital leases and half-corrections for operating leases. As with errors involving stock options, the experiment revealed that auditors put more time into pressing for corrections to numbers in the financial statement than those that were simply disclosed elsewhere.

Based on follow-up interviews, researchers said auditors make their choices knowingly and view misstatements of on-the-books numbers as being more important than those off the books or in footnotes. Since both stock-option and lease accounting are hot-button areas that get a lot of attention, researchers said they expect auditors would be even more tolerant of misstatements for footnoted items involving less important or less controversial items.

Given the findings, the authors said the FASB might consider whether relegating items to footnotes may produce less reliable data, and whether stricter stock-option accounting might have a positive effect in detecting and correcting any errors.

Analysts who crunch numbers from footnotes and other information outside the financial statement also may need to be cautious and understand those results do not produce numbers of the same reliability, the authors warned.

The Wall Street Journal
March 30, 2005
Page 1

Questions for Consideration

1. At the bottom of every page of an annual report's financial statements there is a phrase similar to the following: *The footnotes are an integral part of the financial statements.* To what extent do you believe that footnotes are a reliable part of the financial statements? Discuss.

2. What type of footnote disclosures appear most susceptible to auditors "letting them slide"? Are there any common characteristics to these footnotes? Explain.

Assignment 9
Financing Activities

Name of your company: _____

This assignment focuses on the liability and stockholders' equity sections of the balance sheet. Upon completion, you should have a good understanding of the significant financing activities in which your firm has recently engaged.

Completing the Assignment

1. **Current Liabilities**

   a. Analyze the current liability section of your company's comparative balance sheets. List the two accounts that had the greatest changes since the previous year. Discuss the significance of these changes.

Account	Most Recent Year	Next most Recent Year	Percent Change
_____	$ _____	$ _____	_____ %
_____	$ _____	$ _____	_____ %

   _____

   _____

   _____

   _____

   _____

   b. Is the most recent percentage of your company's assets that are financed with current liabilities significantly different than the next most recent year? Discuss.

   _____ % **Most recent year**

   _____ % **Next most recent year**

   _____

   _____

   _____

   _____

2. **Long-term Liabilities**

    a. Analyze the long-term liability section of your company's comparative balance sheets. List the account in this section that had the greatest change since the previous year. Discuss the significance of the change.

Account	Most Recent Year	Next most Recent Year	Percent Change
_____	$ _____	$ _____	_____ %

_____

_____

_____

_____

_____

    b. Is the percentage of your company's assets that are financed with long-term liabilities significantly different than it was the previous year? Discuss.

        _____ % **Most recent year**

        _____ % **Next most recent year**

_____

_____

_____

_____

Note

A consolidated balance sheet includes all assets and liabilities of a parent firm and its subsidiaries. When a subsidiary is not 100%-owned by the parent firm, some of the subsidiary's assets have been financed (provided) by the subsidiary's other stockholders. Those other stockholders are called minority shareholders. Their ownership interest is usually reported on the consolidated balance sheet between liabilities and stockholders' equity. It is usually labeled Minority Interest or some similar term.

---

3. **Minority Interest**

    a. Did your firm report a Minority Interest?

        _____ Yes   _____ No

b. If yes, indicate the percentage of total assets that are financed (provided) by the minority interest?

_____ % **Most recent year**

_____ % **Next most recent year**

4. **Stockholders' Equity**

a. Study the stockholders' equity section of your firm's comparative balance sheets and the statement of stockholders' equity. List the account that had the greatest change since the previous year. Discuss the significance of this change.

Account	Most Recent Year	Next most Recent Year	Percent Change
_____	$ _____	$ _____	_____ %

_____

_____

_____

_____

b. Is the percentage of the company's assets financed with stockholders' equity significantly different than the previous year? Discuss.

_____ % **Most recent year**

_____ % **Next most recent year**

_____

_____

_____

_____

5. **Overall Summary of Company Finances**

Complete the table below to summarize how your company financed its assets at the most recent balance sheet date and the next most recent balance sheet date. Each column should total 100%.

Source of financing	% most recent year	% next most recent year
a. Current liabilities	_____	_____
b. Long-term liabilities	_____	_____
c. Minority interest	_____	_____
d. Stockholders' equity	_____	_____

6. What amount of cash is the firm obligated to pay out in each of the next five years for repayment of long-term debt, capitalized lease obligations, operating leases, and/or other commitments?

   Hint: *This information usually is contained in the notes to the financial statements and will take careful reading to identify.*

	Repayment of long-term debt	Capital lease obligations	Operating leases	Other commitments
Year 1	$ _____	$ _____	$ _____	$ _____
Year 2	_____	_____	_____	_____
Year 3	_____	_____	_____	_____
Year 4	_____	_____	_____	_____
Year 5	_____	_____	_____	_____
Totals	$ _____	$ _____	$ _____	$ _____

   Average cash commitment in each of the next five years = $ _____

   Average per year cash flow from operations during last 3 years = $ _____

   Does it appear that your firm can cover cash commitments with cash generated by operations? Or will your firm need to raise cash from other sources? Explain.

   _____

   _____

   _____

   _____

   _____

7. Did your firm have any *contingent liabilities* at the balance sheet date? (This information is usually found near the end of the notes to the financial statements.) Discuss the specific nature of these contingencies and how (or whether) they are expected to affect the firm's financial health.

   _____

   _____

   _____

   _____

   _____

   _____

   _____

8. Did your company have preferred stock? _____ Yes _____ No

   Hint: *Look for a preferred stock account in the owners' equity section of the balance sheet. If there is none, skip to question 9.*

   a. _____ Number of preferred shares authorized

   b. _____ Number of preferred shares outstanding

   c. $ _____ Par value of preferred shares

   d. Indicate which of the following features apply.

	Yes	No
Cumulative	___	___
Participating	___	___
Redeemable	___	___
Convertible	___	___
Voting privileges	___	___

   e. For any of the characteristics listed above that apply to your firm's preferred stock, indicate the specifics of that characteristic to your stock. For example, if it is convertible, under what terms can it be converted?

   _____

   _____

   _____

   _____

   _____

   _____

   _____

9. Indicate below whether your firm had treasury stock at the end of the most recent period and/or at the end of the prior period.

   Hint: *Treasury stock is generally deducted as the last item in the owners' equity section of the balance sheet and is reported at cost.*

	Most Recent Balance Sheet	Next Most Recent Balance Sheet	Percent Change
a. Number of shares	_____	_____	_____ %
b. Dollar amount	$ _____	$ _____	_____ %

   c. Is the treasury stock reported at its cost?

   _____ Yes _____ No (If not, skip to No. 10.)

d. Average price paid/share	$ _____	$ _____	_____ %

10. Did your company distribute a stock dividend or implement a stock split during the year?

	Yes	**No**
Stock dividend	___	___
Stock split	___	___

If yes, indicate the size of the stock dividend (e.g., 5%, 20%, etc.) or stock split (e.g., 2 for 1, 3 for 1, etc.) and by how many dollars this action changed the retained earnings balance of the firm during the current year.

	Size	**Change in retained earnings**
Stock dividend	_____	$ _____
Stock split	_____	$ _____

> **Note**
> When a company issues new shares, stockholders often have the *preemptive right* to acquire the new shares in proportion to their present holding and therefore maintain their current percent of ownership. The certificate giving this right is called a *stock warrant*.

11. Does your firm have any stock warrants outstanding? _____ Yes _____ No
    If no, skip to question No. 12.

    a. What is the average stock warrant exercise price at the end of the current year? $ _____

    b. If all stock warrants were exercised, how many shares of stock would be issued? _____

    c. By what percentage would common shares outstanding increase if all stock warrants were exercised? Show your clearly labeled work below.

       _____ %

12. Does the firm have any stock options or share-based compensation plans outstanding? _____ Yes _____ No

    a. How many stock options were exercised during the current year? _____

    b. What was the average exercise price? $ _____

    c. If the cost of stock options was expensed during the most recent year, by how much would net income be reduced (this may be disclosed as a per share amount)? $ _____

    d. What is your company's average exercise/option price? $ _____

    e. By what percent would the number of common shares outstanding increase if all stock options were exercised?

       _____ shares ÷ _____ shares = _____ %

Reading 9/10
Sudden Exposure:
Downside of 'Preferred' Stocks

By Gene Coulter

Tracking the Numbers/
Street Sleuth

The Dividend-Friendly Securities Entice Investors, But Risks Rise With Rates

A guaranteed dividend sounds like a safe investment. Generally, it is – unless it's attached to a preferred stock and interest rates are poised to rise.

Welcome to a corner of the stock market that's little talked about despite the more than $225 billion of these securities outstanding. Preferred securities are much more like bonds than stocks and thus particularly exposed now that the Federal Reserve seems ready to push rates up from historical lows.

Preferred stocks get little attention in part because, in effect, they're stocks in name only. The most basic preferred is sold at a low par price, often $25, and sports a fixed, quarterly dividend. The securities are listed on a stock exchange but don't carry voting rights in the company that sold them. They can be called, or redeemed, by the issuing company, though most preferreds are protected against calls for at least five years from the date they're sold. These characteristics help explain why the stocks tend to trail any rally seen in the common stock of the issuing company. In fact, capital appreciation on preferreds often amounts to very little.

About the only trait that makes preferred stocks, well, stocks, is that many, but not all, are listed as equity on the issuing company's balance sheet.

What preferred stocks do have are those steady dividend payments: They have preference over common stock in the payment of dividends – thus the handle "preferred" – and they also outrank common stock (but trail bonds) in the creditor hierarchy, meaning that preferred shareholders get paid before holders of common stock should the company go bust and still have assets to pay out. There are several types of preferreds, including those that convert into common stock or cash and those sold into trusts then resold to investors. But all of them pay fixed dividends.

It's the steady dividend that entices investors, particularly since changes in the tax code last year made ownership of dividend-yielding securities more attractive. A lot of preferreds have effective yields several percentage points higher than common stocks. Their yields also easily trump those of money-market funds and even better some corporate bonds.

But a sharp rise in rates can hit preferreds where they live: These steady-as-they-go securities can become volatile and lose value. A hit to the security's price can quickly erode the income investors are earning.

Part of the problem is that most preferreds are "perpetual," meaning they have no maturity date and thus carry the interest-rate risk of very long-term bonds.

"This is not an area where you want to tread lightly," says Kurt Reiman, a senior strategist at UBS Financial Services who follows preferred securities and currently recommends clients underweight the sector.

In fact, rates don't even have to move all that sharply by historical standards to blindside preferreds.

Mr. Reiman has put together a "shock analysis" that forecasts what could happen to a theoretical portfolio of debt-by- any-other-name preferred stocks once rates start rising. His analysis assumes securities are held for six months. It shows positive returns for several call dates of preferreds should rates rise only a quarter point. But starting at half a percentage point of rate increases, the wheels start to come off: At that point, preferreds with six months to two years of call protection would produce a total return of 1.81%; those with two years to 3½ years of call protection would lose just over 1%; and preferreds with 3½ to five years of protection would shed 3.8%.

Andrew Montalbano, a preferred-securities trader at Advest, says, "If we go up 50 basis points [or one-half percentage point, in interest rates] you'll see some panic selling."

Yet Mr. Montalbano says it's still a good time for individual investors to buy preferreds, despite potential Fed rate action later this year, because the highest-quality securities are readily available and offer yields that are attractive enough to make up for principal risk. "I think it's a fine time to buy right now, because you get your 7%," Mr. Montalbano says.

Preferreds' principal risk stems in part from the fact that older preferreds offering the highest coupons are also likely to be trading above their $25 par value. These securities also are near their call dates, and upon being called will pay off at par, meaning a shareholder would

lose the difference between the current market price for the security and par.

So, a 7% or 8% yield on a preferred that can be called in 2006 or 2007 effectively is a couple of percentage points lower, but still competitive with a corporate bond offering around 5% or 6%.

Donald Crumrine, chairman of Flaherty & Crumrine Inc., says an investor earning the relatively fat yield premium a preferred offers can afford to take a hit on the price of the security, "but at some point, interest rates will overwhelm." The Pasadena, Calif., firm specializes in preferred securities.

UBS's Mr. Reiman offers an example of how a preferred investor might be able to ameliorate the threat of rising rates by favoring older, more "seasoned" securities. **Household Capital Trust VI** is a high-quality preferred with an 8.25% coupon. Unlike perpetual preferreds, this trust preferred has a maturity — in this case in 2031. But it's also

callable as of Jan. 30, 2006, giving it an effective yield-to-call of 4.70%. That's a better yield than other securities due in 1½ years.

If this sounds like a lot of work for an individual investor, it is. The amount of homework required is just one of many reasons many financial advisers don't recommend preferreds for their clients.

Those who do advise preferreds for their income-oriented clients sometimes recommend closed-end funds, such as those offered by Mr. Crumrine's firm.

One benefit of holding preferreds in a fund is that the funds can use options and other derivatives to manage portfolio risks.

"We don't try to predict rates," Mr. Crumrine says. "We hedge out interest-rate risk."

The Wall Street Journal
May 7, 2004
Page C-3

Steady Rates Preferred

Preferred stocks pay a guaranteed dividend but carry no company voting rights, making them more like bonds – and about as sensitive to interest-rate moves as bonds are. The table below shows how investors holding a range of preferred stocks with different call, or redemption, dates would be affected if rates were to rise over a six-month holding period.

RATE SCENARIO	TIME BEFORE STOCK CAN BE REDEEMED BY ISSUER		
	IN 6 MONTHS TO 2 YEARS	2 YEARS TO 3½ YEARS	3½ YEARS TO 5 YEARS
Current total return	+6.06%	+6.82%	+6.58%
If rates rise ¼ point	+4.10	+3.00	+1.35
If rates rise ½ point	+1.81	−1.02	−3.80

Note: Scenario based on May 6 prices for preferred stocks covered by UNS Financial Services   Source: UBS

Questions for Consideration

1. What are the primary differences between preferred stock and common stock?

2. Do you believe that preferred stock's guaranteed dividend makes preferreds a good investment? Discuss.

Assignment 10
Analysis of Financing Activities

Name of your company: _____

The purpose of this assignment is to evaluate the financing decisions and financing activities which the management of your firm has undertaken.

Key References for this Assignment

- *Mergent Bond Record*, Regent Investors Service (a monthly service),

- *Standard and Poor's Bond Guide* , Standard & Poor's (a monthly service), or

- *The Wall Street Journal*, Dow-Jones, Inc. (published every weekday).

Completing the Assignment

1. Inspect the liability and equity sections of your firm's comparative balance sheets. Does your firm use financial leverage? Is your firm's use of financial leverage greater for the most recent year than for the previous year? If the degree of leverage has changed, what impact has this had on the firm's risk? Discuss.

_____

_____

_____

_____

_____

_____

_____

_____

_____

_____

_____

2. Identify the investment characteristics of your firm's long-term debt. Obtain the most recent monthly issue of either *Mergent Bond Record* or *Standard & Poor's Bond Guide*. (If you have a choice, *Mergent Bond Record* is a little easier to use.) Look up your company to determine whether it has any long-term debt listed. (Companies are listed alphabetically in both publications.) Answer the following questions for each issue of long-term debt. (If your firm has **more** than two issues, select two representative issues for listing here.)

    Not every firm has bonds outstanding, nor are all bonds listed in these sources. If no bond information is available regarding your firm, you may skip this section. (Alternatively, your professor might instruct you to obtain this data for another firm.)

	Long-Term Debt Issue #1	Long-Term Debt Issue #2
a. Type of debt (notes, subordinated notes, senior notes, debentures, etc.)	_____	_____
b. Interest rate	_____%	_____%
c. Year debt is due	_____	_____
d. Debt rating (indicate which rating source you used)		
_____ Mergent	_____	_____
_____ S&P	_____	_____
e. Is the issue "investment grade" or "speculative grade" (i.e. "junk bonds")	_____	_____
f. Call date of the debt (if any)	_____	_____
g. Call price of the debt (if any)	_____	_____
h. Current market price	$ _____	$ _____
i. Recent price range:		
highest price	$ _____	$ _____
lowest price	$ _____	$ _____
j. Yield to maturity	_____%	_____%

3. Identify the primary stock exchange where your company's preferred stock and common stock are traded. (Also, note the ticker symbol, usually a three or four letter abbreviation that identifies the firm's stock.) This information usually is found in the last few pages of the annual report.

    a. Primary stock exchange where your firm's common (and preferred) stock is traded.

    _____

    b. Ticker symbol(s) _____

4. Obtain today's issue (or the most recent issue available) of *The Wall Street Journal.*

   Alternative

   As an alternative go to **www.marketwatch.com**, type in your firm's ticker symbol, and use the category "Quote/News." Skip to c.

   a. Indicate the date of *The Wall Street Journal* that you used. _____

   b. Go to Section C of your issue to find the stock exchange tables. Find your firm's exchange and your firm's data. If your firm has more than one class of common stock listed, select the first one shown. If questions arise about notations in the stock listings, most answers can be found by referring to the "Explanatory Notes" section that usually appears at the bottom of column 1 on page C3 of *The Wall Street Journal.*

   c. Fill in the blank for each of the following.

      1) Price range during prior 52 weeks $ _____ High $ _____ Low

      2) Regular annualized dividend _____

      3) Volume (in hundreds of shares) _____

      4) Day's highest price $ _____

      5) Day's lowest price $ _____

      6) Day's closing price $ _____

      7) Change in price from yesterday $ _____

5. Compute each of the following ratios for your firm for the most recent year.

   a. $\text{Return on (common) equity} = \dfrac{\text{net income (- preferred dividends, if any)}}{\text{(common) stockholders' equity}}$

   $\text{Return on (common) equity} = \dfrac{\rule{3cm}{0.4pt}}{} = \rule{1.5cm}{0.4pt} \%$

Note

Return on equity usually means "return on common equity." Therefore, if a company has preferred stock outstanding, the preferred dividends must be subtracted from the numerator and the preferred stock equity accounts must be subtracted from the denominator. Usually, there are no more than two preferred stock accounts—one for par value and one for paid-in capital in excess of par value. Unless a stockholders' equity account name specifically refers to preferred stock, the account is usually part of common equity.

---

b. Debt to equity = $\dfrac{\text{total debt}}{\text{total stockholders' equity}}$

Debt to equity = —————————————— = ——————— %

c. Debt to assets = $\dfrac{\text{total debt}}{\text{total assets}}$

Debt to assets = —————————————— = ——————— %

d. Dividend payout ratio = $\dfrac{\text{total cash dividends on common stock}}{\text{net income}}$

Dividend payout ratio = —————————————————— = ——— %

e. Current ratio = $\dfrac{\text{total current assets}}{\text{total current liabilities}}$

Current ratio = —————————— = ——————— %

f. Market value to book value per share = $\dfrac{\text{market value per (common) share}}{\text{book value per (common) share}}$

Market value to book value per share = —————————— = ———————

Note

Market value per share and *book value per share* usually refer to common stock. Therefore, to obtain book value per common share:

1. subtract any equity accounts arising from preferred stock from total stockholders' equity, and

2. divide the remainder by the number of common shares outstanding.

---

6. For a ratio to be meaningful it must be compared to that of other companies, or to other years for the same firm. To give some perspective to your firm's ratios, check with five classmates who are evaluating different firms. Place your firm's ratios in the first column and those of your classmates' firms in the other columns.

Alternative

As an alternative to comparing your company's ratios to those of your classmates' companies, you may want to compare with the companies you used in No. 3.e. of Assignment 4. From the financial statement compute the ratios and compare with your company's ratios.

Check with your professor to make sure this option is acceptable.

Ratio	Your Firm	Firm 1	Firm 2	Firm 3	Firm 4	Firm 5
a. Return on (common) equity	_____%	_____%	_____%	_____%	_____%	_____%
b. Debt to equity	_____	_____	_____	_____	_____	_____
c. Debt to assets	_____	_____	_____	_____	_____	_____
d. Dividend payout ratio	_____	_____	_____	_____	_____	_____
e. Current ratio	_____	_____	_____	_____	_____	_____
f. Market value to book value	_____	_____	_____	_____	_____	_____

7. Overall, what does your analysis in Nos. 5 and 6 reveal to you about your firm's liquidity, dividend policy, and use of leverage? Do you observe big differences between your firm and other firms? If you compared your firm to companies in other industries, is there anything about the difference in industry that might tend to explain some of the differences you observed? Discuss.

_____

_____

_____

_____

_____

_____

_____

_____

_____

_____

_____

_____

_____

_____

_____

_____

_____

_____

_____

_____

_____

_____

_____

_____

_____

_____

_____

_____

_____

_____

_____

8. Optional Memo No. 3 – Financing Activities

Your third memo is based on what you have learned about your company's overall *financing activities*.

Guide for Memo No. 3

a. Evaluate your company's financial structure. Include the following:

  ▸ the amount of debt financing and equity financing;

  ▸ the changes from the prior to the current year; and

  ▸ the primary transactions that caused these changes.

b. Based on this additional information about your company's financing, discuss your overall assessment of your company as an investment opportunity at this time.

Name _____   Professor _____

Course _____   Section _____

Assignment 11
Investing Activities

Name of your company _____

In this assignment you will review and evaluate the investing activities in which your company engaged during the most recent year. Generally, investing activities involve the acquisition or disposal of long-term assets.

Completing the Assignment

1. Identify the changes in your firm's long-term asset accounts that occurred during the most recent accounting period. You will probably have to search the footnotes to obtain some of the specific account information requested. Not every balance sheet contains every account listed below. Further, blank lines have been provided for you to write in any additional items that appear in your company's Annual Report or SEC 10-K under long-term assets.

Long-term Assets	Most Recent Balance Sheet	Next Most Recent Balance Sheet	Net Change in Dollars
Long-term investments	$ _____	$ _____	$ _____
Machinery and equipment	_____	_____	_____
Buildings and leasehold	_____	_____	_____
Land	_____	_____	_____
_____	_____	_____	_____
_____	_____	_____	_____
_____	_____	_____	_____
Less accumulated depreciation	_____	_____	_____
Construction in progress	_____	_____	_____
Deferred income taxes	_____	_____	_____
Long-term receivables	_____	_____	_____

(The problem continues on the next page.)

(Continued from the previous page.)

Long-term Assets	Most Recent Balance Sheet	Next Most Recent Balance Sheet	Net Change in Dollars
Excess of cost over net assets of acquired companies (i.e., goodwill)	$ _____	$ _____	$ _____
Other intangible assets	_____	_____	_____
_____	_____	_____	_____
_____	_____	_____	_____
_____	_____	_____	_____
Total long-term assets	$ _____	$ _____	$ _____

These amounts should match the totals on the balance sheet.

2. Inspect the investing activities section of the statement of cash flows and report the following.

	Most Recent Year	Next Most Recent Year
a. Cash spent to acquire long-term assets	$ _____	$ _____
b. Cash received from sale of long-term assets	_____	_____

3. Based on the information in Nos. 1 and 2 above, briefly summarize the significant investing activities, if any, in which your company engaged during the most recent year. Is your firm expanding its long-term asset base? Shrinking it?

_____

_____

_____

_____

_____

_____

_____

_____

_____

_____

_____

_____

_____

_____

4. Identify your firm's accounting policies related to long-term assets.

   Hint: _Most information will be found in the notes to the financial statements._

   a. **Depreciation** – Which depreciation method(s) does your firm use for financial reporting purposes? Check all that apply.

      1) _____ Straight-line

      2) _____ Units-of-production

      3) _____ Declining-balance

      4) _____ Other (specify) _____

      5) If multiple depreciation methods are used, which method is used predominantly? _____

   b. **Investments**

      1) Indicate if your firm owns any securities at the most recent balance sheet date that qualify in the following categories.

         _____ Held-to-maturity securities

         _____ Trading securities

         _____ Available-for-sale securities

      2) Which of these accounting methods were used by your firm to value investments in securities?

         _____ Amortized Cost method (or Cost method)

         _____ Market Value method

         _____ Equity method

         _____ Consolidation method

   c. **Mergers and acquisitions** – Did your firm engage in merger or acquisition activity during the current year or prior year? If yes, describe that activity below.

   _____

   _____

   _____

   _____

_____
_____
_____
_____
_____
_____
_____
_____
_____

d. **Goodwill** – Goodwill is sometimes reported on the balance sheet under a title such as "Excess of cost over fair value of assets acquired."

> **Note**
> Goodwill is no longer amortized over its estimated useful life (not to exceed 40 years). As of a June 2001 change in accounting standards, a company must now test certain intangible assets for "impairment." One of these intangible assets is goodwill. If it is deemed impaired, it must be written down or off.

For the following, use data available for the most recent year.

1) Does your firm report goodwill? _____ Yes _____ No

2) Was goodwill deemed impaired? _____ Yes _____ No

3) Was goodwill written down or off and by how much?

_____ Down $ _____ Amount

_____ Off $ _____ Amount

Reading 11/12
Hidden in Plain Sight

©2005 CFO Publishing Corp.
For more information about reprints from *CFO*, contact PARS International Corp. at 212-221-9595.

By Tim Reason
Senior writer

Leasing may soon have to be justified on economic terms alone.

The Securities and Exchange Commission doesn't like lease accounting, and it's not going to take it any more. In a June report on off-balance-sheet activity commissioned by Congress as part of the Sarbanes-Oxley Act of 2002, SEC staff argued that lease-accounting standards should be rewritten, estimating that they allow publicly traded companies to keep $1.25 trillion (undiscounted) in future cash obligations off their balance sheets.

Released more than eight months late, the report is a testament to the difficulty that even SEC staffers have in gauging the full extent of debt and other obligations that companies can legally keep off their balance sheets.

SEC staffers, who also pushed for changes to pension-plan accounting and for the fair-value reporting of all financial instruments, were sharply critical of the way lease-accounting standards are applied. Currently, the report complains, companies can easily make a financed purchase look instead like a rental contract by "taking advantage of the bright-line nature" of the standards.

The off-balance-sheet treatment that results from such "structuring," it says, has turned leasing into "an industry unto itself" over the past 30 years. "Transparency and the degree to which accounting and disclosure standards achieve their goals can be greatly diminished by the use of structuring, even when that structuring appears to comply with the standards," the report notes. "Leasing is a prime example of this."

Financial Accounting Standards Board chairman Robert Herz, a critic of existing lease accounting, proclaimed his support for the SEC's suggestions in an official FASB release the same day. "My personal view," Herz told CFO two years ago, "is that lease-accounting rules provide the ability to make sure no leases go on the balance sheet. Yet you have the asset and an obligation to pay money that you can't get out of." If companies don't want to capitalize the assets on their balance sheets, he declared, "then something is wrong."

Written in 1976, Fin 13 defines all leases as either capital leases or operating leases. When a company is essentially financing an asset purchase—a capital lease—it records the asset and lease payments on the balance sheet. By contrast, a rental contract—an operating lease—requires neither the asset nor the payment obligation be recorded on the balance sheet.

FLYING WITHOUT WINGS Over the years, that off-balance-sheet treatment has made operating-lease treatment increasingly popular, even for large, essential assets. "Balance-sheet management" appears second on a list of 10 leasing benefits posted to the Website of the Equipment Leasing Association (ELA). The SEC report estimates that only about 22 percent of public companies use capital leases, while 63 percent use operating leases. Yet even more telling are the estimated total cash flows related to noncancelable operating leases, which outweigh the cash flows related to capital leases by more than 25 to 1. As International Accounting Standards Board (IASB) chairman David Tweedie famously observed during Senate testimony after the Enron scandal: "A balance sheet that presents an airline without any aircraft is clearly not a faithful representation of economic reality."

Tweedie's comment is significant: FASB is likely to work closely with the IASB—which has already done several studies on the subject—in developing any new lease-accounting standard.

WHY NOW? Yet not everyone agrees that lease accounting is as serious a problem as the SEC suggests. ELA president Michael Fleming notes that the

81

30-year-old standard has long taken a backseat to more-pressing issues. "No investors are standing up and saying they have been misled because of lease accounting," he says.

Indeed, under an SEC rule adopted in 2003, companies must disclose all contractual obligations—including both types of leases—in a table in the Managements Discussion and Analysis (MD&A) section of the financial statements.

Dennis Hernreich, CFO and COO at Casual Male Retail Group Inc., says lease accounting is "very transparent," and that changes are unnecessary. "To me, there's more than adequate disclosure in the footnotes," he says. Operating leases are, of course, common in the retail industry, where they generally reflect the sort of rental contracts standards setters had in mind. Casual Male's total (undiscounted) future obligation for operating leases of $150 million is disclosed in a table of contractual obligations. (By contrast, Casual Male records $124 million in long-term debt obligations, which appears both in the table and on the balance sheet). Still, if FASB changes the accounting, he says, "we'd have a lot more assets and a lot more liability." But he insists "that really wouldn't be a problem."

Critics of the current accounting acknowledge that off-balance-sheet leases are far less pernicious than the depredations that prompted the SEC report in the first place. But they argue that even sophisticated users don't get all the information they need from the MD&A table, which lays out undiscounted

payments for each of the coming five years and lumps the rest of the lease amount into a "thereafter" category. Charles W. Mulford, an accounting professor at the Georgia Institute of Technology, says even commercial lenders with whom he consults "routinely come up with overly conservative estimates of operating leases."

That's because to find the present value of an operating lease, a financial-statement user must estimate the discount rate, as well as the payment stream for the period beyond five years. (The labor involved is evident in the fact that the SEC itself did not attempt to discount the $1.25 trillion amount in its study.) Moreover, calculating the exact principal and interest for each payment is often complicated by the presentation of costs such as property taxes and maintenance as a lump sum.

"If companies themselves actually do the present-value calculation, it's going to be much more accurate and consistently applied," says Mulford, "than if every user does seat-of-the-pants calculations to figure out what should be on the balance sheet."

WHAT NOW? Lease accounting has already been under pressure in various ways—a recent clarification from the SEC's chief accountant on how to account for certain aspects of property rental led more than 150 retailers and restaurant chains to restate results, while Fin 46 forced many companies to unwind synthetic leases and required companies such as Dell to consolidate vendor-financing arms that themselves issue leases.

But the SEC wants to go further. Its report cites studies by the IASB suggesting lease accounting be based on contractual cash inflows and outflows. Under this method, both the lessor and lessee would report their economic interest in the leased assets, as well as assets and liabilities related to the lease payments. "Leases that are at present characterized as operating leases," notes an IASB summary, "would give rise to assets and liabilities—but only to the extent of the rights and obligations that are conveyed by the lease." This and similar approaches, the SEC report noted, "remain worthy of consideration."

Fleming says the ELA is amenable to change, though it encourages an accounting treatment that is "workable and reflects reality." But, he notes, "you can't treat something on your balance sheet as an asset if you don't own it."

Yet Mulford thinks that's probably exactly what will happen. "A lease on the balance sheet will not represent ownership, but the economic reality of commitment. It won't say you own a [rented] storefront, but that you control it for a certain time, and that it is both an asset and an obligation."

Both sides of any debate already agree on one thing: lease accounting may change, but leasing won't go away. "There are benefits to having use of an asset without owning it," says Geert Kraak, vice president of finance for Dutch Rabobank Group financing subsidiary De Lage Landen. "If you look at how much is financed by leasing companies in the United States and worldwide, that is not just going to disappear. There is a definite need for leasing."

"The value proposition we offer is less and less dependent on the off-balance-sheet treatment of the leases," says Kraak.

"It is more about value added in terms of asset management, risk management, and the availability of point-of-sale financing."

"Accounting treatment was the driving factor for leasing until now," says Dan Sholem, an equipment finance-and-lease ad-

viser. "The SEC's [suggestions] are going to move the emphasis toward the operational benefits of leasing."

CFO
August 2005
Pages 59 - 61

Watch Those Terms

The Securities and Exchange Commission's argument against operating leases is that the accounting often doesn't reflect the true economics of the transaction. But others argue that overzealous pursuit of a favorable accounting treatment actually can cause economic damage.

There is often too much emphasis on the off-balance-sheet treatment, says Dan Sholem, an equipment finance-and-lease adviser. He warns that lack of focus on a company's operational needs can ultimately force it to pay more for leasing an asset than for purchasing it outright. A lot of companies will, at the end of a lease, get stuck with things they wish they'd bought, he says.

Under FAS 13, a lease does not qualify as an operating lease if the company can purchase the asset at a price that is substantially lower than the expected fair value at the end of the lease term. Nor does it qualify if the present value of the lease payments equals or exceeds 90 percent of the asset's fair value. A lease structured to avoid these triggers could cost a company far more than the original cost of the asset if the company later discovers that it needs to buy the asset or extend the lease, says Sholem.

Moreover, he says, the tendency of companies to package multiple big-ticket items into a single lease has complicated subsequent mergers and private-equity buyouts. If there's $50 million of machine tools spread over five facilities and you're buying four facilities, you may have to pay more to buy out equipment you don't need, he notes.

And while finance departments often drive the lease-versus-buy decision, that's not always the case. In equipment-intensive industries, finance executives can sometimes be caught unaware of lease obligations because line managers preferred signing a lease to requesting approval for a large capital expenditure.

Charles W. Mulford, an accounting professor at the Georgia Institute of Technology, also suspects the accounting treatment may drive poor economic decisions. In theory, he says, the benefit of an operational lease is that the lessor can take advantage of economies of scale and the tax benefits of ownership, and pass some of the financial benefit along to a lessee with fewer financial resources. That does happen, he says. But I suspect there are also examples where the inherent cost of funds in an operating lease is higher than a company's actual cost of capital. ✳ T.R.

Questions for Consideration

1. What is the primary criticism of the present accounting for leases? Explain.

2. Go to the web site of Equipment Leasing Association (ELA) referred to in the article: **www.elaonline.com**. Scroll down and click on Choose Leasing. Click on "How leasing helps with cash flow." Read the ten benefits of leasing. Do you believe that the benefits listed would be lost if all leases had to be accounted for as capital leases? Explain.

Assignment 12
Analysis of Investing Activities

Name of your company_____

In this assignment, you will evaluate results of management's investing decisions. First, you will determine selected characteristics of your firm's property, plant, and equipment. Second, you will explore your firm's return on assets by analyzing asset turnover and profit margin. Lastly, you will analyze the profitability of your firm's segments.

Completing the Assignment

1. Evaluate your company's investment in property, plant, and equipment.

   Determine the following amounts as reported by your firm on its most recent financial statements. You will probably have to inspect the notes to the financial statements to obtain some of the information.

   a. Cost of property, plant, and equipment $ _____

   What percent of the cost of property, plant, and equipment was written off as depreciation expense in the most recent year?   _____%

   What does your answer imply about the average life of your company's property, plant, and equipment?

   _____

   _____

   b. Accumulated depreciation $ _____

   What percent of the cost of property, plant, and equipment is in the Accumulated Depreciation account?   _____%

   c. Depreciation expense $ _____

   d. Cash paid for property, plant, and equipment $ _____

   e. On average are the property, plant, and equipment assets relatively new, relatively old, or in mid-life? How did you determine this?

   _____

   _____

   _____

f. What is the relationship between the cost of property, plant, and equipment purchased during the year and the cost of property, plant, and equipment charged to depreciation expense? Does this imply that your firm's productive capacity is growing, getting smaller, or staying about the same? Explain.

_____

_____

_____

_____

2. Evaluate the effect of asset growth on the return on assets.

a. Compute your firm's return on assets for the most recent year.

$$\text{Return on assets} = \frac{\text{net income (- preferred dividends, if any)}}{\text{total assets}}$$

Return on assets = _____ = _____ %

Note

To obtain the most meaningful results, the net income number should *exclude* the effects of special items such as discontinued operations and extraordinary items. If either of these items appear on your firm's income statement for the year under consideration, exclude their impact from net income when making the calculations here and in the parts that follow.

To exclude special items from net income, start with net income, deduct any special items that caused net income to increase, and add back any special items that caused net income to decrease.

---

b. Compute your firm's asset turnover ratio.

$$\text{Asset turnover} = \frac{\text{sales}}{\text{total assets}}$$

Asset turnover = _____ = _____ %

How many dollars of sales were generated by each dollar of assets for the year in question?

$ _____

c. Compute your firm's profit margin.

$$\text{Profit margin} = \frac{\text{net income (- preferred dividends, if any)}}{\text{sales}}$$

Profit margin = _____ = _____ %

For the year in question, how many cents out of every sales dollar did the company keep as profit after accounting for all expenses?

$ _____

d. For perspective, compare your firm's profit margin and asset turnover with those of other firms. Check with five classmates who are evaluating different firms than you are and fill in the table below.

Alternative

As an alternative to comparing your company to those of your classmates, you may want to compare with the companies you used in No. 3.e. of Assignment 4.

Check with your professor to make sure this option is acceptable.

Ratio	Your Firm	Firm 1	Firm 2	Firm 3	Firm 4	Firm 5
		C O M P A R A T I V E F I R M S				
Profit margin	_____%	_____%	_____%	_____%	_____%	_____%
Asset turnover	_____	_____	_____	_____	_____	_____

e. Compared to the other firms, how would you describe your firm's asset turnover and profit margin?

_____

_____

_____

3. Evaluate your firm's segment information.

a. Near the end of the notes to the financial statements you should find information about your company's lines of business. Are your firm's segments all contributing equally to sales and profits? Complete the table of segment information on the following page. List the operating income, identifiable assets, and return on identifiable assets (of each segment) for the current year and two prior years. List the current year information first. (If your firm operates as a single segment, substitute geographic data, if any, in the analysis below.) Divide column A by column B to obtain the return on identifiable assets. To conserve space, record the information in millions of dollars.

Segment Names	Year	(A) Operating Income	(B) Identifiable Assets	(A)/(B) Return on Identifiable Assets
1) _____	_____	$ _____	$ _____	_____%
	_____	_____	_____	_____
	_____	_____	_____	_____
2) _____	_____	_____	_____	_____
	_____	_____	_____	_____
	_____	_____	_____	_____
3) _____	_____	_____	_____	_____
	_____	_____	_____	_____
	_____	_____	_____	_____
4) _____	_____	_____	_____	_____
	_____	_____	_____	_____
	_____	_____	_____	_____
5) _____	_____	_____	_____	_____
	_____	_____	_____	_____
	_____	_____	_____	_____

b. Discuss the results of your segment analysis. Are some segments perform-
ing better than others? Might overall profitability be enhanced by reallocat-
ing assets to some segments and away from others? What questions would
you have for management regarding its various lines of business? Does
management address "segment strategies" in the Management Discussion
and Analysis? Explain.

_____

_____

_____

_____

_____

_____

_____

_____

_____

_____

_____

_____

_____

_____

_____

_____

_____

_____

_____

_____

_____

_____

_____

_____

_____

_____

_____

_____

_____

4. Optional Memo No. 4 – Investing Activities

Now that you have completed Assignments 11 and 12, you are prepared to write the fourth memo based on your company's *investing activities*.

Guide for Memo No. 4

a. What can you conclude about the company's investment policies based on its investment activities?

b. What were the primary causes for the change in fixed or long-term assets from last year to the current year?

c. What new insights do you have relative to your assessment of the company?

d. Discuss whether or not you are now more favorably impressed with your company.

Assignment 13
Operating Activities

Name of your company _____

The purpose of this assignment is to review your company's annual report and SEC 10-K information regarding its operating activities. Because operating activities have the greatest effect on the income statement and current assets, those items will receive special attention.

Completing the Assignment

1. Describe the revenue recognition method(s) used by your firm. If the notes to the financial statements are silent on this topic, your firm probably recognizes revenue at the point of sale.

   _____

   _____

   _____

   _____

   _____

   _____

   _____

   _____

2. Effective management of receivables is critical for most firms. The change in receivables should be consistent with the change in sales. Provide the following detailed information regarding sales, accounts receivable, and allowance for bad debts, also known as "allowance for uncollectible accounts."

   Hint: *Some of this detail may be listed in the notes to the financial statements.*

(The assignment continues on the next page.)

	End of Most Recent Year	End of Next Most Recent Year	Percent Change
a. Sales revenue	$ _____	$ _____	_____ %
b. Gross accounts receivable	_____	_____	_____
c. Less allowance for bad debts	_____	_____	_____
d. Net accounts receivable	_____	_____	_____
e. Allowance for bad debts as a percentage of sales	_____ %	_____ %	
f. Allowance for bad debts as a percentage of ending accounts receivable	_____ %	_____ %	

g. Are the percentage changes in accounts receivable and allowance for bad debts similar to the change in sales or are they different? Discuss the implications of any differences you observe.

_____

_____

_____

_____

_____

_____

_____

_____

_____

_____

Note

Not all firms have inventories. Companies that provide services instead of goods will not have significant inventory, e.g., banks, insurance companies, electric power companies and airlines.

As the United States moves to a more service-based economy there are more and more companies such as Federal Express (package delivery services) and H&R Block (income tax preparation services) that do not have inventory.

Attention: *If your firm is primarily a service firm, you may skip Nos. 3 and 4. Ask your professor if he/she wishes you to substitute another firm's data for this section of the assignment.*

3. Effective management of inventory is also critical for most firms. Changes in the levels of inventory should be consistent with changes in the level of cost of goods sold. Provide the following detailed information regarding cost of goods sold and the various categories of inventory.

   Hint: *Some of this detail may be listed in the notes to the financial statements.*

	End of Most Recent Year	End of Next Most Recent Year	Percent Change
a. Cost of goods sold	$ _____	$ _____	_____ %
b. Merchandise inventory	_____	_____	_____
c. Raw materials inventory	_____	_____	_____
d. Work in process inventory	_____	_____	_____
e. Finished goods inventory	_____	_____	_____
f. _____	_____	_____	_____
Total inventories	$ _____	$ _____	100 %

   g. Is the change in total inventories (and the change in each component of inventory) similar to the change in cost of goods sold or different? Discuss the implications of any differences you observe.

   _____

   _____

   _____

   _____

   _____

   _____

   _____

   _____

   _____

   _____

   _____

Note
The Dollar-value LIFO, Retail LIFO, and Retail Dollar-value LIFO methods in No. 4 are merely specialized applications of the basic LIFO method you have learned about in accounting class.

4. Which inventory valuation methods are used by your firm? (Mark all that apply.)

   Hint: *This information usually is provided in the first note to the financial statements. Remember, service firms probably won't have inventories.*

   a. _____ Weighted-average

   b. _____ FIFO

   c. _____ LIFO

   d. _____ Dollar-value LIFO

   e. _____ Retail LIFO

   f. _____ Retail Dollar-value LIFO

   If more than one method is used, does one method predominate? _____

   If so, indicate that method. _____

5. Did your firm disclose any subsequent events? If so, describe the subsequent event(s) that occurred and explain why this is important information that needs to be disclosed.

   Note
   Subsequent events are important events or information that come to light after the balance sheet date but before the financial statements are distributed. They are usually disclosed in the notes to the financial statements.

   _____
   _____
   _____
   _____
   _____
   _____
   _____
   _____
   _____

Reading 13
The ones that get away

The Economist

Accounts are increasingly more art than science

It is corporate earnings season once again, and investors are poring over the numbers. This week, Sprint, an American telecoms firm, announced net profits more than twice as high as a year ago. Amazon, an internet retailer, revealed net income that had fallen by 32%, due, the firm said, to tax issues. The shares of both companies rose. Should they have done?

Profits figures are meant to shed light on how a company—and its stock price—might fare in the future. But many experts worry that increasingly they don't. The scandals at Enron and WorldCom—as well as more recent accounting snafus at General Electric and a big scam at AIG—show that accounting numbers are malleable. And they are getting squishier as the use of estimates in company accounts increases.

Whether this malleability is a problem is the subject of heated debate and carries with it important consequences. Reliable numbers mean that investors can make sound decisions. Bad ones lead not just to the inefficient allocation of capital but also to a loss of confidence in the markets and, when fraud is involved, to huge shareholder losses. A study by Glass Lewis, a research outfit, found that investors lost well over $900 billion in 30 big scams between 1997 and 2004.

Ever since accounting shifted from the simple tallying of cash in and cash out to "accrual accounting", where profits and expenses are booked when incurred, forward-looking estimates have played a critical role in measuring company profits. This role has grown as "knowledge-based" economies have begun to replace the old widget-making versions, and businesses have become more complex.

The biggest boost to estimation, however, has come from the gradual shift to "fair-value" accounting. Before, assets and liabilities were mostly carried at their historic, original cost; "fair value" is an attempt to show their current worth. Fair-value numbers are up-to-date and arguably more relevant than their static but verifiable precursors. But they also result in more volatile profits and a heavier reliance on estimates for the many items (bank loans, buildings) that may not have a ready market.

Standard-setters on both sides of the Atlantic have been urging this shift. In June America's Securities and Exchange Commission, in a long-awaited report commissioned by Congress after the Enron scandal, also endorsed fair-value accounting, which it thinks will simplify accounts and reduce firms' interest in structuring transactions to meet accounting goals.

Others are less sanguine. Even with the best will in the world, estimates can be wildly off the mark. And they are easy to manipulate. In a recent study, Daniel Bergstresser and Mihir Desai of Harvard Business School and Joshua Rauh of the University of Chicago's Graduate School of Business found ample evidence of tinkering. At delicate moments—before acquisitions and equity offerings and exercising stock options, for example—some bosses inflated the assumed rate of return on pension-fund assets, thus flattering profits.

Baruch Lev of New York University's Stern School of Business, and Siyi Li and Theodore Sougiannis, from the University of Illinois at Urbana-Champaign, harbour a deeper worry: that estimates, which are supposed to improve the relevance of financial information by giving managers a means to impart their forward-looking views (on how many customers might return their new cars, for instance), are not very useful at all. That is, they do not really help investors to predict a company's future earnings and cash-flows.

The three analyzed 3,500-4,500 companies a year from 1988 to 2002. They then tried to "predict" future performance (earnings or cashflow) with five models in which historic cashflows and estimates were used to different degrees. The trio found that cashflows predicted future performance robustly, but adding estimates to them was little help in predicting future performance, or in generating returns from portfolios based on these predictions. It was a "sobering result", they concluded.

Mr Lev blames this on the difficulty of making good estimates in a fast-changing, complex world as well as on a degree of earnings manipulation. "This is not to say we should toss the accounting system, which is overwhelmingly based on estimates, into the waste bin," he says, "but it does point to the urgent need to enhance the reliability of accounting estimates—especially given the move to fair value."

On this point, even proponents of fair value agree. The Financial Standards Accounting Board (FASB), America's standard-setter, is planning to release guidance on how to apply fair value later this year. It has devised a "hierarchy" of items according to how hard they are to value. At the top are items that have an observable price in a deep, liquid market (e.g., listed corporate debt). In the middle are items where sophisticated valuation models are based on market inputs (e.g., employee

stock options). At the bottom are items where valuations are based wholly on management projections (e.g., Enron's most esoteric financial instruments).

It is the lower end of the hierarchy that causes concern. "At this level, there is the risk that models can be used with prejudice," says David Bianco of UBS, a Swiss bank. Regulators, too, are worried. Research by the Federal Reserve shows that the fair value of bank loans can swing widely depending on inputs and methodology. Market values for lower-rated corporate bonds, one possible benchmark, can vary by as much as 2-5%, giving managers leeway to fiddle with numbers.

The objective is objectivity

"Estimates are part of accounting. So the focus shouldn't be on the number of estimates," argues Neri Bukspan, chief accountant at Standard & Poor's, a ratings agency, "but rather the objectivity and independence of those making the estimates and those tasked with verifying them." This puts a greater onus on auditors to weed out good estimates from hyped ones—making their independence even more critical than it seemed after Enron. The Public Accounting Oversight Board, recognizing this, also plans to expand its audit guidance on fair value.

Investors need to scrutinize

the numbers harder, too. Better disclosure would help them. Mr Lev suggests that firms should say how much of key reported figures is based on facts (e.g., revenues in the bag) and how much on estimates—a proposal that companies claim would tip their hand to competitors. But both FASB and its international counterpart are drafting standards requiring increased disclosure of how fair values are derived and their impact on profits and balance sheets.

Mr Lev has a more ambitious proposal. This entails forcing management to periodically "true up"—that is, disclose how their previous estimates have panned out. He argues that this would inject discipline into the system, allowing investors to penalize companies that consistently make bad estimates. Lynn Turner, a former chief accountant at the SEC, agrees. "Markets can't discipline without transparency." Defenders of fair value say that this is confusing and unnecessary. A change in estimated value could be due to changing market conditions, not to a bad estimate. And fair-value accounting itself, some argue, is a constant "true up". But then, there's "true" and true.

The Economist
July 30, 2005
Pages 65 - 66

Questions for Consideration

1. What makes financial statements "squishy"? Explain.

2. Assuming fair-value accounting supplants historical cost accounting as GAAP, what can be done to minimize the estimation issue? Explain.

Assignment 14
Analysis of Operating Activities

Name of your company _____

The purpose of this assignment is to determine the effects of management's operating decisions. You will (1) identify your firm's profit strategy, (2) evaluate your firm against selected measures of efficiency and effectiveness, and (3) link your firm's operating and investing activities with financing activities.

Completing the Assignment

1. Which profit strategy does your firm appear to be following: product differentiation or cost leadership? To help answer this question, compute your firm's return on assets and its two component parts: profit margin and asset turnover. Use the most recent year's data available.

   a. Return on assets = profit margin × asset turnover

   OR to expand the factors of the ratio:

   1) $$\text{Return on assets} = \frac{\text{net income}}{\text{operating revenues}^*} \times \frac{\text{operating revenues}^*}{\text{total assets}}$$

   *means the same as "sales"

   Note

   Be sure to use an income number that excludes the effects of special items that are not expected to recur. For example, this means that items such as discontinued operations and extraordinary items should be excluded from the income number you use.

   ---

   2) Return on assets = _____ × _____

   3) Profit margin = _____ %

   4) Asset turnover = _____ %

b. For perspective, compare your company's profit margin and asset turnover to the results of your classmates who are studying different firms than you are. Fill in the table below.

Attention: *If you completed the table in No. 2.d. of Assignment 12, skip to c.*

Alternative

As an alternative to comparing your company to those of your classmates, you may want to compare with the companies you used in No. 3.e. of Assignment 4.

Check with your professor to make sure this option is acceptable.

	Your Firm	COMPARATIVE FIRMS				
		Firm 1	Firm 2	Firm 3	Firm 4	Firm 5
Profit margin	_____%	_____%	_____%	_____%	_____%	_____%
Asset turnover	_____	_____	_____	_____	_____	_____

c. While more than one year's data would be needed for a complete analysis, what does the foregoing data suggest to you regarding your firm's profit strategy as compared to the other firms? Which firms appear to be following a cost leadership strategy? Which firms a product differentiation strategy? Do any firms appear to be doing a little of both, or not much of either?

_____

_____

_____

_____

_____

_____

_____

_____

_____

_____

_____

_____

_____

_____

_____

_____

_____

2. Compute the following measures of efficiency and effectiveness for your firm.

    a. Operating cash flow to total assets $= \dfrac{\text{cash flow from operations}}{\text{total assets}}$

        Operating cash flow to total assets $=$ ——————————— $=$ _____ %

    b. Inventory turnover $= \dfrac{\text{cost of goods sold}}{\text{inventory}}$

        Inventory turnover $=$ ——————— $=$ _____

    c. Accounts receivable turnover $= \dfrac{\text{operating revenues (sales)}}{\text{accounts receivable}}$

        Accounts receivable turnover $=$ ——————————— $=$ _____

    d. Gross profit margin $= \dfrac{\text{operating revenues - cost of goods sold}}{\text{operating revenues}}$

        Gross profit margin $=$ ———————————————— $=$ _____ %

    e. Operating profit margin $= \dfrac{\text{operating revenues - all operating expenses}}{\text{operating revenues}}$

        Operating profit margin $=$ ———————————————— $=$ _____ %

    f. Return on equity $=$ profit margin $\times$ asset turnover $\times$ financial leverage

        Return on equity $=$ profit margin $\times$ asset turnover $\times \dfrac{\text{total assets}}{\text{equity}}$

        Return on equity $=$ ————— $\times$ ————— $\times$ ————— $=$ _____ %

                              $\begin{bmatrix} \text{take from} \\ \text{No. 1.a.3)} \end{bmatrix}$ $\begin{bmatrix} \text{take from} \\ \text{No. 1.a.4)} \end{bmatrix}$

3. For perspective, compare your company's ratios to the results of your class-mates who are studying different firms than you are. Fill in the table as before.

   Alternative

   As an alternative to comparing your company to those of your classmates, you may want to compare with the companies you used in No. 3.e. of Assignment 4. Check with your professor if this option is acceptable.

	Your Firm	**Firm 1**	**Firm 2**	**Firm 3**	**Firm 4**	**Firm 5**
		C O M P A R A T I V E F I R M S				
Operating cash flow to total assets	____%	____%	____%	____%	____%	____%
Inventory turnover	____	____	____	____	____	____
Accounts receivable turnover	____	____	____	____	____	____
Gross profit margin	____	____	____	____	____	____
Operating profit margin	____	____	____	____	____	____
Return on equity	____	____	____	____	____	____

4. Assuming the current year's ratio values are representative, where is your company strong in relation to the other firms and where is it weak?

   _____

   _____

   _____

   _____

   _____

5. Optional Memo No. 5 – Operating activities

   You have completed Assignments 13 and 14 and now have sufficient knowl-edge to prepare the fifth memo based on your company's *operating activities*.

   ## Guide for Memo No. 5

   a. What can you conclude about your company's operating activi-ties? Are they becoming more or less profitable?

   b. Did any expense significantly increase or decrease relative to sales?

   c. Discuss whether your company's operating activities make you more or less excited about your company.

Reading 14
For Annual-Report Purposes, Hurricane Katrina Is 'Ordinary'

By Diya Gullapalli

Tracking the Numbers/Outside Audit

Extraordinary events are unfolding in the aftermath of Hurricane Katrina, but for financial-reporting purposes they will be considered "ordinary."

The distinction pales in comparison to the human suffering and vast property damage along the Gulf Coast. In coming months, though, the issue could take center stage, as U.S. companies seek to assess damages and costs for their quarterly and annual financial filings.

Accounting officials say extraordinary items should be just that—extraordinary. They take a separate line below income from continuing operations on a company's income statement, segregated from costs that are part of normal business operations. Many analysts and investors exclude such extraordinary items when assessing a company's results, and so make the results look better or worse.

For an event to be considered extraordinary, accounting rules say it must be "infrequent in occurrence" and "unusual in nature." Even the terrorist attacks of Sept. 11, 2001, didn't meet those criteria, according to a task force of the Financial Accounting Standards Board, the accounting rule-maker for U.S.

publicly traded companies. The FASB's Emerging Issues Task Force found it impossible to separate the direct financial and economic effects of the attacks from the prevailing economic conditions before the event and the impact on the economy afterward. Members also noted the potential for future attacks.

The FASB plans to take a similar line with Katrina, which is believed to have killed hundreds or thousands of people and caused billions of dollars of damage.

"As tragic as hurricanes and other natural disasters are for everyone affected, unfortunately every year many businesses across the country are affected by these types of events and thus they do not represent an unusual and infrequent occurrence to businesses or to insurers," wrote FASB spokesman Gerard Carney in a statement responding to a question.

In general, accounting authorities are loath to let companies chalk up losses as extraordinary, because the practice can lead to companies' blaming all sorts of costs on one event. The FASB task force next meets in mid-September and could choose to look into the issue more closely.

The rules for what counts as extraordinary long have been tough. One accounting textbook

terms them "so restrictive" that they can include only "such items as a single chemist who knew the secret formula for an enterprise's mixing solution but was eaten by a tiger on a big game hunt or a plant facility that was smashed by a meteor."

As for events often referred to as acts of God, where they occur is a big factor. So, for example, while a frost damaging orange crops in Florida wouldn't qualify as extraordinary, one damaging wheat in Kansas may. When Mount St. Helens erupted in 1980, Weyerhauser Co. reported a $36 million loss of timber, logs and building equipment as extraordinary largely because such an eruption hadn't occurred at the volcano in 130 years.

But six hurricanes hit the U.S. last year, and two have hit this year. Many touched the Gulf Coast, and more are likely to do so in the future. On top of that, New Orleans is below sea level, and so always has been a candidate for severe flooding. According to one tutorial from an accounting professor in Columbia, Mo., "A flood in a flood plain is not extraordinary, but one on a mountain would be."

The almost-Biblical level of flooding in New Orleans seems to push this hurricane closer to the realm of extraordinary for accounting purposes—but it still may not qualify.

"There will be people who will argue or question whether this is extraordinary, but the bigger debates will be about the size of various losses," says Doug Tanner, a partner in PricewaterhouseCoopers LLP's risk and quality group.

"Maybe the severity of what's going on in Mississippi, Alabama and Louisiana is infrequent, but that in itself doesn't make it an unusual occurrence," says Carl Kampel, a member of the FASB task force. He said companies could explain costs and losses in footnotes.

The Wall Street Journal
September 2, 2005
Page C-3

Questions for Consideration

1. How would you explain to someone who does not have an accounting background that the losses from Hurricane Katrina could not be categorized as an "extraordinary item" for financial reporting purposes?

2. If a company could measure its loss(es) from Katrina, how would the loss(es) be reported in the company's financial statements? Explain.

Assignment 15
Capstone Project/Optional Final Memo

The purpose of this assignment is to integrate the information you have obtained about your company and industry into a coordinated report. The report is to be typed and have a professional appearance. You should assume that your first post-college employer has asked you to research the firm you've been working on during this course. He/she may be considering your firm as a potential supplier, customer, competitor, or acquisition candidate. Your employer may even be secretly entertaining an offer of employment from this firm. Under any of these circumstances, you will want to present your employer with a carefully- researched, thoughtfully-written, and professionally-presented document.

Completing The Assignment

In general, unless modified by your professor, you have great flexibility in completing this assignment. For example, you may choose any organization structure for this report that you believe best captures and presents the necessary information. You should be creative and complete in your analyses and presentation. Generally, your report is to be based on the assignments you have completed during this course as part of the **Annual Report Project** (**ARP**). In some cases, however, you will want to include additional information or additional creative analysis that is especially important to understanding the financial health and status of your firm (or firms) and industry. Where appropriate, you should prepare charts or graphs to illustrate the facts you present.

Keep in mind that your employer may put your report to a variety of uses. For example:

▸ If your assigned firm is a prospective supplier, your employer would want to assess its long-run stability and its continuing ability to provide quality goods at reasonable prices.

▸ If your assigned firm is a potential customer, your employer will be concerned with its ability to meet its short-term obligations as they become due.

▸ If your assigned firm is a candidate for investment, your employer will want to understand its long-term financial structure, cost structure, and profit structure.

Your report should be flexible so that it can be used in any of these ways. Regardless of the format you use, your report must include a summary section that states your overall assessment of the financial health and status of your firm. For example, is it strong, weak, improving, or deteriorating? Would you make a short-term loan to this firm? Would you make a long-term loan to this firm? Would you buy stock or invest your career with this company? Discuss why or why not.

1. **Suggested Outline** – If you are unsure how to organize your report you might consider the following outline. It follows the assignment structure of the **ARP**. If you completed Assignment 7, begin here with Part e.

   Important: *Be sure to check with your professor to determine if he/she has specific guidelines regarding the organization of your report.*

   a. Basic Company Information

   b. The Company's Economic, Social, Legal and Political Environment

   c. Industry Information

   d. Overview of the Annual Report, SEC 10-K and Proxy Statement

   e. Financing Activities

   f. Investing Activities

   g. Operating Activities

   h. Summary Statement on Financial Health and Status of the Company

   If you use this suggested outline, be careful that you don't merely make lists of the information that you collected on the assignment sheets of the **ARP**. The outline format of the assignments is very efficient for recording the data you found for your company, but it won't be very helpful to your employer. Remember, your employer hasn't read the articles or consulted the references that you have. You will be expected to provide greater background, detail, analysis and commentary than what appears in your completed assignments.

2. **Due Date(s)** – To be announced by your professor.

3. **Annual Report**, **SEC 10-K**, and **Proxy Statement** – If you have not already done so, provide each of these documents to your professor when you turn in your report.

> **Note**
> If you are part of a team in which each member is researching a different firm, avoid the temptation to write a separate report for each company and staple the reports together. Instead, this report should be an *integrated* report in which the firms are compared, contrasted, and summarized in each section. Your report must focus on comparisons and contrasts among the firms and on an integrated assessment of the overall industry situation. You will be expected to provide greater background, detail, and analysis than what appears in your individual completed assignments.

4. Optional Memo No. 6 – Final Recommendation

If you have completed the first five memos, your professor may want you to prepare a final memo to complete the **ARP**.

Guide for Memo No. 6

a. Make your final recommendation to your client.

 Briefly highlight significant information from previous memos to emphasize your point.

 Include industry trends which could affect your company in the near future.

b. End your memo with a paragraph about the thoroughness of your firm in preparing information for your client and give one or two reasons why your new firm should continue to advise your client.

Appendix A
Accounting Synonyms

One of the perplexing aspects of learning accounting is that there is so much variation in terminology. Often, two or more terms mean exactly (or very nearly) the same thing. If you don't recognize a particular term, look it up here. You may have already learned the concept or principle under a similar or different name.

Accounting Term

Alternative Accounting Terms

A

Accounting Term	Alternative Accounting Terms
Acid-Test Ratio	Quick Ratio
Accounting Equation	Basic Accounting Equation; Balance Sheet Equation
Accounting Rate of Return	Simple Rate of Return
Allowance for Bad Debts	Allowance for Doubtful Accounts; Allowance for Uncollectible Accounts
Allowance for Doubtful Accounts	Allowance for Bad Debts
Allowance for Uncollectible Accounts	Allowance for Bad Debts
Annuity	Ordinary Annuity
Asset	Unexpired Cost

B

Accounting Term	Alternative Accounting Terms
Bad Debts Expense	Uncollectible Accounts Expense
Balance Sheet	Statement of Financial Position; Statement of Financial Condition
Balance Sheet Equation	Accounting Equation; Basic Accounting Equation
Basic Accounting Equation	Accounting Equation; Balance Sheet Equation
Basket Purchase	Lump-sum Purchase (or acquisition); Joint Purchase; Group Purchase
Bearer Bond	Coupon Bond
Book of Original Entry	Journal; General Journal
Book Value	Carrying Value
Burden	Factory Burden; Overhead; Manufacturing Overhead
Business Entity Concept	Entity Concept; Separate Entity Concept

C

Accounting Term	Alternative Accounting Terms
Capital Stock	generic term for either common or preferred stock
Carrying Value	Book Value
Cash Discount	either a Sales Discount or Purchase Discount, depending on the circumstances
Cash Value	Fair Value; Fair Market Value; Market Value
Cash Equivalent Value	same as Cash Value
Charge an account	Debit an Account
Closely Held Corporation	Nonpublic Corporation
Common Stock	Capital Stock
Constant-Dollar Accounting	Price-Level Accounting; GPL Accounting
Contract (Interest) Rate	Stated Rate; Coupon Rate; Nominal Rate; Face Rate
Continuity Principle	Going Concern Principle
Contributed Capital	Paid-In Capital
Contribution Approach to Pricing	Variable Approach to Pricing

Coupon Bond	Bearer Bond
Coupon (Interest) Rate	Stated Rate; Nominal Rate; Face Rate; Contract Rate
Current Cost Accounting	Current Value Accounting
Current Ratio	Working Capital Ratio
Current Value Accounting	Current Cost Accounting

D

Debenture Bond	Unsecured Bond
Differential Cost	Incremental Cost
Direct Costing	Variable Costing
Direct Labor Efficiency Variance	Labor Efficiency Variance; Labor Usage Variance; Direct Labor Usage Variance
Direct Labor Price Variance	Direct Labor Rate Variance
Direct Labor Rate Variance	Labor Price Variance; Direct Labor Price Variance; Labor Rate Variance
Direct Labor Usage Variance	Direct Labor Efficiency Variance
Direct Materials Quantity Variance	Materials Quantity Variance; Materials Usage Variance; Direct Materials Usage Variance;
Direct Materials Usage Variance	Direct Materials Quantity Variance

E

Earnings	Income; Profit
Earnings Statement	Income Statement; Profit and Loss Statement
Effective Interest Rate	Market Rate; Yield Rate
Entity Principle (or concept)	Separate Entity Principle (or concept); Business Entity Principle (or concept)
Expense	Expired Cost
Expense and Revenue Summary account	Income Summary account
Expired Cost	Expense

F

Face (Interest) Rate	Stated Rate; Coupon Rate; Nominal Rate; Contract Rate
Face Value (of bonds or notes)	Par Value; Maturity Value; Principal
Factory Burden	Burden; Overhead; Manufacturing Overhead
Fair Market Value	Fair Value; Cash Value; Market Value
Fair Value	Fair Market Value; Cash Value; Market Value
Financial Leverage	Leverage; Trading on the Equity
Fixed Assets	Plant Assets; Productive Assets; Tangible Assets; Property, Plant and Equipment
Freight-In	Transportation-In

G

Going Concern Principle	Continuity Principle
General Journal	Journal; Book of Original Entry
General Price-Level Accounting	Price-Level Accounting; Constant-Dollar Accounting; GPL Accounting
General Price-Level Gain/Loss	Price-Level Gain/Loss
GPL Accounting	General Price-Level Accounting; Price-Level Accounting; Constant-Dollar Accounting
Gross Margin (on sales)	Gross Profit
Gross Profit (on sales)	Gross Margin
Group Purchase	Basket Purchase; Lump-sum Purchase; Joint Purchase

H

High Yield Bond	Junk Bond; Speculative Grade Bond
Hurdle Rate	Minimum Desired Rate (of return)

I

Income	Earnings; Profit
Income Statement	Earnings Statement; Profit and Loss Statement
Income Summary account	Expense and Revenue Summary account
Incremental Cost	Differential Cost
Internal Rate of Return	Time Adjusted Rate of Return
Inventory	Merchandise Inventory

J

Joint Purchase	Basket Purchase; Lump-sum Purchase; Group Purchase
Journal	General Journal; Book of Original Entry
Junk Bond	High Yield Bond; Speculative Grade Bond

L

Labor Efficiency Variance	Direct Labor Efficiency Variance
Labor Price Variance	Direct Labor Price Variance
Labor Rate Variance	Direct Labor Rate Variance
Labor Usage Variance	Direct Labor Efficiency Variance
Leverage	Financial Leverage; Trading on the Equity
Lump-Sum Purchase	Basket Purchase (or acquisition); Joint Purchase; Group Purchase

M

Manufacturing Overhead	Overhead; Burden; Factory Burden
Marketable Securities	Temporary Investments; Short-term Investments
Market (Interest) Rate	Effective Rate; Yield Rate
Market Value	Fair Value; Fair Market Value; Cash Value; Current Value
Materials Quantity Variance	Direct Materials Quantity Variance
Materials Usage Variance	Direct Materials Usage Variance
Maturity Value (of bonds)	Face Value; Principal; Par Value
Merchandise Inventory	Inventory
Minimum Desired Rate (of return)	Hurdle Rate
Monetary Unit Principle	Unit-of-Measure Principle
Mortgage Bond	Secured Bond

N

Net Earnings	Net Income; Net Profit
Net Income	Net Profit; Net Earnings
Net Profit	Net Income; Net Earnings
Nominal Account	Temporary Account
Nominal (Interest) Rate	Stated Rate; Coupon Rate; Face Rate; Contract Rate
Nonpublic Corporation	Closely Held Corporation
Normal Operating Cycle	Operating Cycle

O

Operating Cycle	Normal Operating Cycle
Ordinary Annuity	Annuity
Ordinary Bonds	Term Bonds

Overhead   Manufacturing Overhead; Burden; Factory Burden
Owners' Equity   Shareholders' Equity; Stockholders' Equity

P

Paid-In Capital   Contributed Capital
Partnership Agreement   Partnership Contract; Articles of Co-Partnership
Par Value (of bonds)   Face Value; Principal; Maturity Value
Periodicity Principle   Time-Period Principle
Permanent Account   Real Account
Plant Assets   Fixed Assets; Property, Plant and Equipment;
                                                Productive Assets; Tangible Assets
Preferred Stock   Capital Stock
Price-Level Accounting   Constant-Dollar Accounting; GPL Accounting;
                                                General Price-Level Accounting;
Price-Level Gain/Loss   General Price-Level Gain/Loss
Principal (of bonds)   Face Value; Maturity Value; Par Value
Productive Assets   Plant Assets; Property, Plant and Equipment;
                                                Fixed Assets; Tangible Assets
Profit   Income; Earnings
Profit and Loss Statement   Income Statement; Earnings Statement
Property, Plant and Equipment   Plant Assets; Fixed Assets; Productive Assets;
                                                Tangible Assets
Purchase Discount   Cash Discount

Q

Quick Ratio   Acid-Test Ratio

R

Real Account   Permanent Account

S

Sales Discount   Cash Discount
Secured Bond   Mortgage Bond
Separate Entity Principle   Entity Principle (or concept); Business Entity Principle
Shareholders' Equity   Stockholders' Equity; Owners' Equity
Short-term Investments   Temporary Investments; Marketable Securities
Simple Rate of Return   Accounting Rate of Return
Speculative Grade Bond   Junk Bond; High Yield Bond
Stated (Interest) Rate   Coupon Rate; Face Rate; Nominal Rate; Contract Rate
Statement of Financial Condition   Balance Sheet; Statement of Financial Position
Statement of Financial Position   Balance Sheet; Statement of Financial Condition
Stockholders' Equity   Shareholders' Equity; Owners' Equity

T

Tangible Assets   Fixed Assets; Plant Assets; Productive Assets;
                                                Property, Plant and Equipment
Tax Avoidance   Tax Planning
Tax Planning   Tax Avoidance
Temporary Account   Nominal Account
Temporary Investments   Short-term Investments; Marketable Securities
Term Bonds   Ordinary Bonds
Time Adjusted Rate of Return   Internal Rate of Return
Time-Period Principle   Periodicity Principle

Trading on the Equity   Leverage; Financial Leverage
Transportation-In   Freight-In

U

Uncollectible Accounts Expense   Bad Debts Expense
Unexpired Cost   Asset
Unit-of-Measure Principle   Monetary Unit Principle
Unsecured Bond   Debenture Bond

V

Variable Approach to Pricing   Contribution Approach to Pricing
Variable Costing   Direct Costing

W

Working Capital Ratio   Current Ratio

Y

Yield (Interest) Rate   Market Rate; Effective Rate

112

Appendix B
Common Acronyms

While reading annual reports, particularly in the notes, you may find acronyms with which you are not familiar. The acronyms most commonly found in annual reports are listed here.

Acronym	Identification
AICPA	American Institute of Certified Public Accountants
AMEX	American Stock Exchange
CEO	Chief Executive Officer
CFO	Chief Financial Officer
COO	Chief Operating Officer
COSO	Committee of Sponsoring Organizations
CPA	Certified Public Accountant
EBIT	Earnings Before Interest and Taxes
EBITDA	Earnings Before Interest, Taxes, Depreciation and Amortization
EITF	Emerging Issues Task Force
EPS	Earnings Per Share
ESOP	Employee Stock Option Plan
EVA	Economic Value Added
FAS	Financial Accounting Standard
FASB	Financial Accounting Standards Board
FCF	Free Cash Flow
FIFO	First-in, First-out
FSP	FASB Staff Positions
GAAP	Generally Accepted Accounting Principles
GAAS	Generally Accepted Auditing Standards
GASB	Government Accounting Standards Board
IARS	International Accounting Reporting Standard
IAS	International Accounting Standard
IASB	International Accounting Standards Board
IT	Information Technology
LCM	Lower-of-Cost-or-Market
LIFO	Last-in, First-out
LLC	Limited Liability Company
LLP	Limited Liability Partnership
MD&A	Management Discussion and Analysis
NASDAQ	National Association of Securities Dealers Automated Quotation
NYSE	New York Stock Exchange
OPEB	Other Post-employment benefits
PACOB	Public Accounting Oversight Board
P (and) L	Profit and Loss Statement
PE	Price Earnings Ratio
PV	Present Value
PVFP	Present Value of Future Payments
R&D	Research and Development
ROE	Return on Equity
ROI	Return on Investment
S&P	Standard and Poors

SAB	Staff (SEC) Accounting Bulletin
SARs	Stock Appreciation Rights
SEC	Securities and Exchange Commission
SFAS	Statement of Financial Accounting Standard
SOP	Statement of Position
SPE	Special Purpose Entity

Notes

Notes

Notes